CATCHING THE KNOWLEDGE WAVE?

THE KNOWLEDGE SOCIETY AND THE FUTURE OF EDUCATION

JANE GILBERT

NZCER PRESS
Wellington 2005

NZCER PRESS
New Zealand Council for Educational Research
PO Box 3237
Wellington
New Zealand

Reprinted 2006, 2008

ISBN 1-877398-01-3
ISBN 978-1-877398-04-9

NOTE TO READER

To avoid cluttering the text with references and footnotes, I have put all citations together in a notes section at the end of each chapter. Readers who are interested in finding out more about any of the ideas mentioned in the text can follow up these citations. The full references are given in the list at the end of the book.

Design
Cluster Creative

Printed by Printlink
Wellington

Distributed by NZCER Distribution Services
PO Box 3237
Wellington
New Zealand
www.nzcer.org.nz

CONTENTS

CHAPTER 1

SCHOOLS, KNOWLEDGE, AND THE FUTURE

OVER THE LAST FEW YEARS, WE HAVE BEEN HEARING A lot about something called the knowledge society. Knowledge and learning, once education's domain, are now a key focus of business and government, and we are supposed to be striving to become a knowledge-based society. But what *is* a knowledge-based society? Do we *want* to be one? What, if anything, does all this have to do with schools? Should schools be contributing to this? Or should they be resisting it? Why? This book explores these questions. It argues that the term knowledge society is a kind of shorthand for a completely new set of ideas about knowledge—what it is, how it develops, how it is used, what it is for, and who owns it. These new ideas challenge many of the assumptions our schools rest on, so much so that if we *do* want to be a knowledge society, we are going to have to change much of what we do in schools.

Why is this? Should we care? As a way of exploring these questions, I want to tell a couple of stories from a recent book by an American journalist called Michael Lewis. In his book, called *Next: The Future Just Happened*, Lewis argues that we are in the midst of a "status revolution", a revolution in traditional understandings of authority and knowledge, and that this revolution has something to do with the Internet. Lewis interviewed a 14-year-old boy who became something of a media celebrity after setting himself up as a share trader on the Internet. He bought shares, recommended them to other investors, using a Yahoo bulletin board, and when their value rose, he sold them, usually the same day, and usually for a significant profit. Within a year, this boy turned an initial investment of $8,000 into $800,000. Eventually, however, the US Securities and Exchange Commission (SEC) took an interest in his activities and formally charged him with stock market fraud. The basis of the SEC's case against the boy was that he "used fictitious names" (four different email addresses) and "manipulated" the stock market: that is, he artificially raised the prices of shares by subjecting them to something other than "ordinary market forces". The rules the boy had apparently violated were put in place when the SEC was created in the 1930s to regulate the behaviour of professional investors. This boy was clearly not a financial professional: he had no formal qualifications and no formal knowledge of how to play the game of stock market trading. He just went ahead and did it. The people who read his bulletin board and acted on his tips presumably found them convincing and useful, but because his tips had "no basis", the SEC argued he was "acting fraudulently".

Lewis says that this story hit the headlines because the boy's activities exposed some important flaws in the SEC's rules. In particular, it exposed their assumption that "high finance" is an activity properly carried out, not by ordinary people, but by the members of a professional élite, an exclusive gentlemen's club. The boy's age, the fact that his activities took place in his bedroom in an ordinary suburban house, using an ordinary computer and an ordinary email account, and the fact that he used his earnings to buy a Mercedes SUV (that he was not old enough to drive) violated not only the SEC's official rules but also their sense of what was right and proper. This boy was doing what financial professionals do every day and, despite no formal initiation into the rules of the game, he was, on the Internet, able to convince people of the usefulness of the information he provided. The SEC's case against him was, in the end, not upheld: the only fraud he committed was in not being who the people who used his tips *probably* thought he was. As Lewis puts it, the boy invented himself on the Internet. He used the fact—probably obvious to any adolescent—that the line older people see between "reality" and "perception" is, on the Internet, quite blurred. When people saw this boy in person, they treated him like a 14-year-old boy. However, when they saw his thoughts on financial matters on the Internet, they treated him as a serious trader, which, for all intents and purposes, he was. The boy told Lewis that he enjoyed being "taken seriously" and treated as if he "was someone". As Lewis says, "on the Internet, where no one could see who he was, he became who he was."

The second story from Lewis's book that I want to tell here is that of another boy, this time 15 years old, who set himself up as a legal advisor, also using only an email account. This boy regularly answered hundreds of questions a day, some of which were from people who were obviously in serious legal trouble. On the website he used, he quickly became the third most highly rated expert in criminal law, ahead of over 100 qualified lawyers, as well as many ex-police officers and several ex-convicts, all of whom were over 30. When interviewed by Lewis, the boy said that he did not "usually" research the answers he gave, that he thought books were "boring", and he very definitely did *not* like reading. He said he "just knew" the answers. His mother said that she thought he had a "gift"—that he had been "born with" the knowledge. When pressed, the boy did say that he occasionally looked at various legal websites. He also said that he had probably learned much of what he knew from watching television shows about the law (he gave the show *Judge Judy* as an example).

In his book, Lewis also outlines the development of Napster and Kazaa (peer-to-peer file-sharing software that allows people to download music from other people's computers rather than buying it), and the invention of text messaging by Finnish adolescents. His point is that these innovations are the work of adolescents. A second point is that all the boys he describes were "outsiders" in some sense or another. Most were not doing especially well at school, and most were loners who did not fit especially easily into the social networks that were available to them. However, he says, each of these boys had refused to accept the status assigned to him — dumb or uncool. Rather, each was actively constructing his own story about his future. As one of the boys explained, in the digital world, he could be "on the same level" as people who, out in the "real" world, would be unlikely to speak to him.

Lewis found the activities of these boys interesting for two main reasons. First, if they—and other people—are using the Internet to play with their identity, then this is probably because they find the identities available to them in the real world inadequate in some way. Second, these boys have detected an important shift in people's attitudes to, and understandings of, knowledge. The development of the Internet has made it possible for people to look for knowledge *wherever it might be found*. They no longer have to wait for those who supposedly possess the knowledge to provide it. The boys Lewis describes were able to reinvent themselves as knowledge providers. That they did this so successfully forces us to think very carefully about what knowledge *is*. The boys' activities undermine the status of those who are supposed to provide us with knowledge. They call into question traditional ideas about formal training and qualifications, and undermine the authority and professional standing of the people who have them.

The activities of these boys became news stories because they are deeply disturbing to existing forms of authority. They also unsettle most people's understanding of knowledge and identity. As Lewis points out, before the Internet, it would have been very difficult for these boys to construct themselves as (highly successful) knowledge providers. However, while the Internet allowed them to do the things they did, it did not *cause* them. It isn't that simple. What Lewis is saying is that these boys had, at some level, grasped the fact that traditional forms of knowledge—and the identities and authority that go with them—are on the way out. They have passed their use-by date and are, says Lewis, "ripe to be challenged". The boys' activities were not random events. Nor did they take place because technological developments made them possible. They took place because there was, according to Lewis, "a social hole to be filled". They are part of (and are contributing to) the development of a wider social phenomenon, a *zeitgeist*, or spirit of the times.

Some educationists will respond to Lewis's stories by arguing that we need to make more effort to engage boys like these in school activities—by developing better teaching methods, by presenting the curriculum in more interesting ways (using ICT, for example), or by developing the boys' social skills. Others might say that the boys' activities are part of popular culture or that they are just adolescent games—practice for, but distinct from, real life. The real game of adult life is a game that has established ways of doing things, ways that have to be learned (from older experts) before one is qualified to participate.

I think these views miss the point of Lewis's stories. Focusing on finding ways to be more inclusive or to better discipline these boys restates the debate within its current terms. Lewis's stories tell us that we need new terms (and a new debate). Lewis picked out these stories, not because he is especially interested in the stock market, the law, or the music industry, nor because he is especially interested in the activities of adolescent boys, but because he thinks that the boys' activities are evidence that we are in the midst of a revolution—a major social and intellectual revolution. Something very important is happening here, something that we need to take notice of and respond to, and something that we cannot understand from within our usual frames of reference. We need to think in new ways, but before we can do this, we need to dig down below the surface of our old ways of thinking—to see how they work, and how they could be different.

In this book, I argue that we should see the changes Lewis describes not as a threat, but as an important opportunity to rethink some of what we do in schools—and why we do it. In our current system, we try (at least in theory) to include and discipline everyone, but we are not especially successful. We have educational experts who decide what is best for all of us—what we should learn, when we need to learn it, and how it is best for us to learn it. Those who "have what it takes" assimilate this material, and all that goes with it, while the rest are "unsuccessful" and either drop out or go into remedial programmes designed to help them "measure up".

Two key ideas underpin our current way of doing things: *knowledge* and *individuality* (or personhood). Most of us assume that these ideas have particular meanings that are obvious and beyond question. However, in the new order Lewis alerts us to, these ideas are developing new and completely different meanings. This new order has a variety of names. Depending on the context, it is known variously as post-modernism, post-industrialism, the knowledge society, the knowledge age, or the knowledge economy. To keep things simple, I'll call it the knowledge society, even though doing so glosses over a large and complex academic debate.

A defining feature of this new order is that new and very different ways of thinking are challenging and replacing long-standing and highly significant ways of thinking. These changes do not represent the usual process of adding to and improving existing ideas: rather they represent a paradigm shift—a radical break with the past that requires us to stop and completely rethink much of what we do. In the following pages, I'll outline the new ideas about knowledge and individuality, and explain how they differ from the old. I'll look at why they are significant for schools, and suggest some approaches for redeveloping our schools so that they can prepare our young people for life in the knowledge society.

Why is this book necessary? Aren't our policy makers and school administrators already onto this? How did I come to be writing about this? I am an educational researcher who worked as a secondary school teacher of science for about 10 years, and then as a university lecturer (for another 10 years). As a university lecturer, I taught educational sociology and philosophy. It was my job to teach people about different theories of knowledge—what people in different historical periods, different cultures, and different intellectual disciplines think knowledge is—and how these ideas are taken up in different educational contexts. So, when I began to read about the knowledge society in the news media, and when our government sponsored a major project and two conferences on something called the Knowledge Wave, I took a great deal of interest. It was clear to me straight away that the term knowledge, when it is used as part of terms like knowledge society or knowledge wave, meant something quite different from what educators or philosophers of knowledge (and ordinary people) might mean when they use this term.

At about the same time as the first Knowledge Wave conference, I attended a Ministry of Education seminar in which several OECD officials reported on a Ministry-commissioned evaluation of the New Zealand education system. At this seminar, one of the officials wondered why it is that knowledge society ideas are extremely influential in business and government around the world, yet have had almost no impact on what goes on in schools. I thought this was a very interesting question. Why is it, I asked myself, that educators are taking very little notice of these ideas? Is this a good thing or a bad thing? If we are supposed to be turning ourselves into a knowledge society, shouldn't our education system be playing a major role in this? Knowledge is, after all, the core business of schools and all other educational institutions. Are educators just too busy, or are they not interested? Do they think that these ideas are part of the business world and therefore nothing to do with them? Or are they a bunch of conservative Luddites who insist on holding on to outdated ideas from the past, even though their job is to prepare young people for the world of the future? Are they intentionally resisting these ideas? Are they defending some important ideals that are absolutely central to Western civilization as we know it? Or is something else going on?

When I read the material from the Knowledge Wave conferences and saw how the term knowledge was being used, I wasn't puzzled any more. I realised that the knowledge society advocates and the educators were talking past each other, largely because they were using the term knowledge to mean quite different things. But *do* educators need to have a better understanding of the "new" view of knowledge? And do business and policy people need to better understand what *educators* mean by knowledge? Perhaps we should just expect these two very different groups to have different languages. However, the conferences made it clear that many people see education as the solution to the problems we face as we try to become a knowledge society. As such, then, these two groups of people *do* need to understand each other. If they fail to engage with one another in relation to these developments, I think we will see the marginalisation and eventual decline of our public education system. Education will increasingly become a matter for individuals and their families, and society as a whole will become more and more polarised. The more I thought more about this, the more it became clear to me that this is an important moment in time. We have, right now, an opportunity to break away from certain entrenched positions of the past and to approach some of public education's most intractable problems in new ways.

I decided to explore these ideas further. I began to read everything I could find about the knowledge society. I read policy documents and books on business management. I read media stories and popular literature, and anything I could find on the future of schooling. I found that there is a large literature on the knowledge society and a large literature on the future of education. There are numerous policy documents in this area, mostly focusing on how to improve our education system's overall performance, and how to tweak the system to better meet 21st century human resource needs.

The work written for teachers and teacher educators mostly looks at what schools will be like in the future. According to this literature, the schools of the future will be managed very differently, and will look very different. They will be multi-campus entities, offering multi-layered, individualised programmes of learning. Students will be able to select elements from these programmes and to move in and out of them in whatever ways best suit their needs. Schools will be learning brokers, matching students with whoever or whatever they need at any given point in time, and they will work closely with other agencies and community organisations to do this. Specialist schools will offer programmes tailored to the needs of particular niche markets. Some will focus on sport, science, the arts, or technology, and others on meeting particular learning needs, or the needs of particular cultural groups. The curriculum will be more integrated (fewer boundaries between the different subjects) than it is now, and there will be a strong emphasis on developing thinking, learning, and problem-solving skills, on creativity, and on the ability to work collaboratively in teams. The use of information and communications technology (ICT) will be routine.

As well as this work on the future of schools, there is an academic literature (still quite small) that is critical of education policy responses to the knowledge society, particularly the failure to acknowledge that knowledge-based economies, if left unregulated, tend to exacerbate existing inequalities and exclusions. Other work criticises what it sees as the conceptual confusion of recent policy.

The literature on the future of schools I found particularly interesting. However, as I read it, it struck me that the writers lacked a sense of knowledge's new meaning. Nor could I find mention of the implications this new meaning might have for schools. The writers seemed to be assuming that a knowledge-based society is one in which there is *more* (and possibly *better*) knowledge, but that this knowledge will be more or less the same kind of knowledge that we have now. The writing confirmed for me that people seem to think a knowledge-based society is one in which knowledge is more important than it is now, or that it is one that emphasises scientific or technological knowledge, or knowledge of ICT.

The schools literature contains a great deal of talk about learning, about how it will be different and better in the schools of the future. However, there is very little talk about *what* students might need to learn. The dominant view seems to be that it doesn't really matter what students learn, as long as they are learning something. Because knowledge is growing so fast and areas of it being replaced so quickly, schools can't be expected to provide people with all the knowledge they will need when they leave school, but they can provide them with some basic learning skills. Because we can no longer expect to stay in the same job, or even the same kind of work, for the whole of our working lives, we now need to be life-long and self-regulated learners. Learning *how* to learn, and learning to identify one's individual learning style, are now key focuses of schooling.

Learning how to learn is, of course, extremely important. But, the way I see it, learning has to involve learning something, and it matters what this something is. *What* people learn, and what they *do* with what they learn, is extremely important, not only because it makes a difference to their ability to get a good job, but also because it makes a difference to their ability to contribute to society.

If we, as educators, fail to engage with these ideas, we can expect to see some already present trends intensify. There will be more emphasis on education's utilitarian function (sorting and credentialing people for the job market), and less emphasis on its social justice function. We will hear louder criticisms of public education's "failures", and louder calls for the public education system to be "rolled back" and left to "the market". On the other hand, if we simply take on board everything the proponents of the knowledge society tell us, we can expect a similar result. The approach I argue for in this book is one that takes knowledge society ideas into account, but uses them strategically in ways that aim to preserve education's traditional links with social justice and social cohesion. A key argument in this approach is the idea that *knowledge matters*.

The history of educational development—in this country and others—is littered with examples of well-intentioned policy initiatives that have failed, largely because they didn't mesh well with the public's understanding of the issue. Before we can redevelop our education system for the knowledge society, we need a new public agreement about what we want from our education system. If this agreement is to work, we must precede it with informed public debate that considers where we have come from *and* where we want to go.

As we think about what our schools will be like in the new order, we need to engage with the new understandings of knowledge. The current policy emphasis on learning and improving the overall performance of our national education system is important, but focusing on this alone will *not* increase our ability to compete on the world economic stage, or to survive as a viable sovereign state. If we are to build this country into a high-skills, high-wage economy with high levels of social cohesion, we require, at the very least, policies that ensure everyone has an equal opportunity to succeed.

My aim in this book is to contribute to the debate. I argue that, although we need to rethink some of the assumptions our education system rests on, and to do some things differently, we do not need to invent many of the tools, ideas, and resources that we will need. They are out there already—in schools, in the community, and in the educational literature. What I think we do need, however, is a coherent framework for putting these ideas together, one that is underpinned by a clear and generally accepted understanding of what it is we want to achieve.

This book is a hybrid. Some of the ideas in it come from the reading outlined above. Other parts of it come from research I did for my PhD. Many of the ideas I discuss originate from scholarly work that, on the surface, appears to have little to do with education—philosophy, media, and cultural studies, political theory, sociology, and business management for example. I also draw on popular culture and the news media, on my experience as a secondary school and, later, university teacher. While I at times call on ideas from academia in this book, I have not written it for a purely academic audience. Nor I have set out to provide a detailed road map of practical strategies for teachers. Rather, I have tried to write in a way that makes the issues accessible for people who work in education, and for those who don't, but who care about the future of education in this country. The focus of the book is very much on ideas.

The academic ideas that have influenced the structure of this book derive from a body of work known as post-modern theory. Post-modernism obviously means "coming after" modernism. The term as generally used refers to a historical period beginning somewhere in the mid to late 20th century and characterised by major social, intellectual, and economic changes. One of these changes, as already mentioned, is that knowledge is changing its meaning. However, many of our other "big ideas" are also changing. For example, some of our most basic political concepts—democracy, equality, ethics, justice, and so on—are developing new meanings. Traditional oppositions—between left and right, local and global, the public sphere and the private, and between "popular" and "high" culture—are becoming less and less relevant. The goal of establishing a common ground, a unified "one best way" that all can live by, is being replaced with a new emphasis on diversity, multiple positions and voices, on *many* ways to do things, make meaning, and just *be*. Linked with this is an emphasis on living (well) with difference, on listening for and working with difference (rather than trying to assimilate it), and on new ways of understanding individuality (or what it means to be a person). The idea of people as self-contained, individual, thinking "subjects" is giving way to a focus on relationships, synergies, and connectedness, and on language's role in constructing, rather than simply representing, meaning.

Before considering how these ideas tie in with notions of knowledge and the implications of these notions for schools, I take a closer look (in Chapter 2) at the knowledge society. I outline what the knowledge society is, where it has come from, and what it is replacing. I explore a number of questions. How and why does the knowledge society involve a change in knowledge's meaning, and changes to the way we work? What are the implications of all this for New Zealand? And for our schools? To understand exactly why these changes are such a challenge to our current education, we need to know something about how this system developed. What drives it? What is it supposed to achieve? Why is it supposed to do this?

In Chapter 3, I briefly look at some of the ideas and events that gave us our current education system. Starting with Plato, the chapter looks at early ideas about what education is for, and how these ideas changed with the advent of mass education and the industrial age. It ends by exploring why we need to rethink some of these ideas as we move into the knowledge age.

Chapter 4 explores, in a little more depth, the "mental models" of knowledge, mind, and learning that underlie industrial age approaches to education. It looks at how and why these models arose, why they are so difficult to change, and why they need to change if we are to develop a knowledge-age education system. The chapter outlines some recent work (in cognitive science) that challenges these models, and suggests some practical approaches for building new ways to think about knowledge, learning, and minds.

Chapter 5 shifts the focus away from knowledge onto politics. Here, I argue that while it is important to understand the new models of knowledge, we also need to take account of certain other developments. I outline the new ideas about individuality, identity, and equality that link with the new ideas about knowledge. I look at how and why these changes are important for education and suggest some ways we could build some of these ideas into what we do in schools.

In Chapter 6, I argue that taking on board post-modern ideas about knowledge and individuality does not, as some have claimed, mean that "anything goes" or that "nothing matters"' any more. In this chapter, I set out why I think that knowledge still matters, why I think that what people learn in our schools matters a great deal, and why I think that the "old" disciplines will still be important. I argue that we need a new, educationally appropriate theory of knowledge, and, along with this, teaching approaches that emphasise the big picture and the ability to *do* things with knowledge.

In the final chapter (7), I summarise the book's main ideas and suggest some ways we could begin to put them into practice in schools.

NOTES

Pages **4-8:** Michael Lewis book is called *Next: The Future Just Happened* (New York, W. W. Norton, 2001). The words in quotes on pp.4-8 are taken from this book.

Pages **10–11:** The first Knowledge Wave conference was held in 2001 and the second took place in 2003. For information on the Knowledge Wave conferences see the website: www.knowledge wave.org.nz. The Ministry of Education seminar I refer to on p.11

took place in March 2001 and was called *Knowledge Management in the Learning Society.*

Pages **12-14:** The New Zealand policy literature on the future of education is strongly influenced by the OECD work in this area - see especially the document *Knowledge Management in the Learning Society* (OECD 2000). Some recent policy documents outlining the government's vision for education in the knowledge society are as follows: *Growing an Innovative New Zealand* (Prime Minister's Department 2000); *Briefing for the Incoming Minister of Education* (Ministry of Education 2002); *People and Capability* (Ministry of Education 2001); *The New Zealand Talent Initiative: Strategies for Building a Talented Nation* (LEK Consulting 2001); *New Zealanders: Innovators to the World* (Science and Innovation Advisory Council 2001); *The Knowledge Economy* (Information Technology Advisory Group 1999); and the documents on the Knowledge Wave website (www.knowledgewave.org.nz).

Beare (2002) and Hargreaves (2004) are two recent works that look at what schools will be like in the future. Codd et al. (2001) and (Australian) Commonwealth Department of Education, Training and Youth Affairs (2000) contain recent reviews of research and other literature on the future of schooling.

For work on the knowledge society's links with increasing inequality, see Brown (2003); Brown and Lauder (2001); Brown, Green and Lauder (2001); or Gee Hull and Lankshear (1996). For philosophical critiques of the education policy response to the knowledge society, see Peters (2001a, 2001b, 2002, 2003).

Pages **15-16:** Tyack and Cuban (1995); Fullan (1993); and Tyack and Tobin (1994) discuss the difficulties in achieving genuine reform in education. McKenzie (1992); Openshaw, Lee and Lee (1993) and Openshaw (1995) discuss various policy initiatives in New Zealand's educational history that failed or were only partially successful because they were not well understood or supported by the general public. There are of course many more recent examples that are yet to be formally documented – the curriculum reforms of the 1990s, and the introduction of the NCEA being obvious examples.

Historians of education (see for example, Grace 1990; Dale 1991; Openshaw 1995) often write about the form of a country's education system at any given point in time as being the result of a 'settlement' or policy consensus. By this they mean a shared set of understandings about the nature and purpose of education which is supported by the various stakeholders in education, including students and their parents. This settlement usually develops out of some sort of "crisis" that has necessitated the negotiation of new agreements between different stakeholders and their—often conflicting—sets of ideas. If this settlement is largely consistent with current government policy and political ideals, current institutional structures, current professional knowledge, and current public opinion, then it is likely to be stable and productive. If, on the other hand, it is not widely supported and has significant internal contradictions, it is likely to precipitate a further "crisis", with the result that its life will be short and unproductive. According to Roger Openshaw, our national education system was, until recently, dominated by what he calls "the New Zealand post-primary settlement" (Openshaw 1995). This consensus, he argues, goes back fifty (now sixty) years to the Thomas Report and Peter Fraser's 1939 statement to Parliament about equal educational opportunity and a "comprehensive, broad and balanced education for all". It was disrupted by the reforms of the 1990s and we have not, as yet, developed an enduring replacement. Knowledge Society developments, because they directly challenge current institutional structures, current professional knowledge, current public understandings of education's purpose, and, to some extent, current educational policy, are likely to precipitate the kind of crisis described by Openshaw et al. Before we can usefully respond to these developments, it is, it seems to me, clear that we need a new policy settlement.

CHAPTER 2

THE KNOWLEDGE SOCIETY: WHAT IS IT?

OVER THE LAST FIVE YEARS OR SO, MOST OF US HAVE probably noticed the term knowledge appearing in places we wouldn't have expected to see it a decade ago. We have government policies that want us to "catch the knowledge wave", the media is full of talk about the knowledge economy, the knowledge revolution, and smart cities, and business discussions are peppered with terms like knowledge management, knowledge resources, knowledge clusters, knowledge work, and knowledge workers. However, most of us have probably not noticed how this proliferation of new terms is changing knowledge's meaning. The new meaning of knowledge is very different from the one most of us use in everyday conversation. It is also very different from traditional philosophical understandings of knowledge. Because of this, it represents a major challenge to education as we currently know it.

Knowledge's meaning used to be the province of philosophers. Philosophers studied and talked about knowledge—what it is, how it develops, and so on. The rest of us, while we all used, acquired, and maybe even created knowledge, didn't think much about what it meant to do these things, or about how we could do them better. In the 1970s, sociologists began to study knowledge. They looked at the creation and use of knowledge from the point of view of the people who do it, and at how and why some forms of knowledge come to be valued more highly than others. More recently, however, knowledge has been taken over—first by cognitive scientists and then by the business world—and philosophers no longer own it. Knowledge is now the subject of intense interest in the business world. We have knowledge-creating companies, the knowledge-based economy, and the knowledge society. The result of all this is that knowledge no longer means what it used to.

This chapter looks at how and why the meaning knowledge is changing. What *is* the knowledge society? Why are knowledge and learning being talked about so much by people in business and government? How can something as basic as knowledge change its meaning, and what does this mean for schools?

In the large number of academic books and articles written on the subject, the term knowledge society means the patterns that are emerging as countries move from the industrial to the post-industrial age. Knowledge (or intellectual capital), we are told, has replaced other more tangible assets like labour, land, and money as the key driver of economic growth. Where industrial societies were based on extracting and using natural resources in manufacturing, knowledge societies are based on developing and exploiting new forms of knowledge. The shift from one to the other is linked with a major decline in blue-collar forms of employment and an increase in job opportunities in the creative, technology, and service-based industries. It is also aligned with new business practices and patterns of work.

The knowledge society is also associated with developments in ICT and globalisation. Our ability to digitise all kinds of information (including money) and to move it around the world at enormous speed has produced major socio-political change. People's understandings of time, space, and place are changing, and the boundaries between countries are breaking down. We are developing new forms of information, new ways of presenting information, and new forms of money. There are new, much more complex, forms of personal identity, and people are connecting with one another in new and different ways.

Knowledge societies are *not* societies that value knowledge more than other societies. *All* societies value knowledge. Nor, as some people seem to think, are knowledge-based societies those that need *more* people who know a lot—in the traditional sense. Rather, they are societies in which people see knowledge in *economic* terms, as the primary source of all future economic growth. However, and this is important for the purposes of this book, the knowledge that is to drive this growth is not knowledge as most people understand it: it is something quite new and different.

To understand how this fundamental change in meaning has come about, we need to know something of the social, political, and economic circumstances that gave knowledge the meaning most of us still have for it, and to know something of the circumstances that are now giving it new meaning.

FROM THE INDUSTRIAL AGE TO THE KNOWLEDGE AGE: CAPITALISM OLD AND NEW...

In the way the story is usually told, the industrial age begins with the industrial revolution (in late 18th century England and France). The industrial revolution came about because of a revolution in knowledge. Before the industrial revolution practical forms of knowledge were not usually written down, but were passed on through apprenticeships. This kind of craft-based technical knowledge was only available to a select few, specialists who fiercely protected it through guilds and other trade-based organisations.

However in the period, known as The Enlightenment, just before the industrial revolution in Europe, there was a major focus on collecting, organising, and publishing a wide variety of different practical forms of knowledge in order to make it widely available. This had a major effect. As this knowledge became available and began to circulate, it was easier for people to use, build on and improve the work of others—especially work from fields outside their own. The result was that there was a period of massive technological innovation. This period, now known as the industrial revolution, was also a period of major social and political change. England in particular changed a great deal. From being a primarily rural, agriculture-based society, it became a highly urbanised, industrial, and very wealthy society. This wealth made

England a major imperial power, which went on to generate significant further wealth using resources taken from its overseas colonies.

Two major innovations were a feature of the industrial age. These were the production-line method of manufacturing and the bureaucratic model of management. The production line, wherein the process of manufacturing something is broken down into steps, made it possible to produce a wide range of standardised goods on a very large scale, using relatively unskilled workers. Bureaucratic, or "top down", styles of management developed as a way of organising the very large enterprises made possible by this form of manufacturing.

Industrial age production systems need two kinds of employee—workers and managers. Workers are people hired to carry out the highly specific tasks involved in one small step of the overall production process. If production is to be efficient, these people need to be reliable, punctual, and respectful of those in authority over them. They need to be able to follow instructions, to understand simple rules and procedures, and to carry out their tasks within prescribed time limits. They do not need to understand the overall production process, take responsibility for anything other than their own work, or think for themselves. Managers, however, are expected to understand and supervise the organisation's work systems and to relay instructions from its top-level managers to its workers in a form the workers can understand. This two-tier system of management was so efficient in increasing productivity (there was a 50-fold increase in one 80-year period) that it was widely adopted as the model for managing all medium- to large-scale organisations, including those, such as government organisations, that do not manufacture anything.

While the industrial age model of production proved to be a very good way to produce standardised consumer goods on a large scale, its efficiency was the basis of its demise. Production capacity quickly outstripped demand, especially when, first the Japanese, and then other emerging industrial nations, began to produce cheaper, and eventually better, versions of the same goods. The saturation of world markets with the kinds of goods that can be made using industrial age methods produced a crisis in international capitalism that led, in the latter part of the 20th century, to new forms of capitalism, known as "fast" capitalism. These involve new methods of production, products, and ways of working. They are associated with new occupational categories, new forms of identity, and new ideas about knowledge, and they are the basis of the knowledge society.

FAST CAPITALISM, INNOVATION, AND CHANGE

The key word in fast capitalism is innovation. The industrial age focus on mass producing standardised goods for standardised markets has been replaced by a focus on constantly developing new products for small, diverse, and increasingly sophisticated niche markets. Because world markets for standardised products are saturated, and any new product appearing on the market can be quickly be copied and produced more cheaply by another company (probably from a part of the world that has cheap labour), competition for new markets is intense. If businesses are to survive in this context, they must constantly innovate. Their products must be easily customisable for the needs and preferences of individual customers. If the business is to grow, it must create new, previously unknown needs and preferences—that it can then meet with its new products. (A commonly given example of this is the Sony Walkman's development from the portable tape recorder.) Today, in post-industrial-age capitalism, the emphasis is on branding, developing niche products (especially cultural and media products), and adding value to existing products. The strong growth in the media and image production industries has produced a significant new occupational category, referred to by some commentators as the "creative class". And despite the predictions of the early information age theorists, big cities are not dying, but are increasingly important as vibrant, knowledge-rich centres of diversity. Face-to-face interaction is even more important to business than it was in the industrial age.

In post-industrial societies, people's social identities are formed, not via their work or their socio-economic status, as they were in the industrial age, but by their patterns of consumption—by the market segments they occupy and the brands they choose. We live in a culture dominated by images, sound bites, and fragmentary ideas that, because of their rapid turnover, can never settle or be properly processed. Difference, novelty, change, and choice are valued over standardisation, stability, and external authority. Elements from global culture sit side-by-side with local symbols, which often take on new meanings as a result. Where the old forms of capitalism provided people with a common dream to aim for and so favoured social cohesion, the new forms of capitalism foster the individualising of desire, which is, according to some commentators, producing a decline in social cohesion.

The focus on innovation has had some interesting spin-offs. Innovation, in a business context, is a form of creative destruction. To innovate is to remake an old product in new ways for a new market (and to get it into that market before one's competitors). This remaking means that the old product is superseded and forgotten. Linked with this view of innovation are new ideas about quality. Quality is no longer a measure of the reliability or durability of products, but of *change*, of continuous improvement (as expressed in the Japanese concept of *kaizen*), and innovation. A quality product is not one that does the job it was designed to do: it is one that, by being new and different, creates a new market.

This emphasis on change has had another interesting effect. Industrial-age companies focused on their *products*. Their aim was to improve the quality of their products so that their customers would buy more of them. They emphasised *things*, and the properties or attributes of things. In contrast, fast capitalism businesses focus on how to *change* things. They study the contexts, processes, and systems in which a thing functions or is used in order to find *new* functions or uses for it. The knowledge needed by fast capitalism businesses is thus very different from the knowledge that industrial-age businesses need. The new businesses need knowledge of how to make things *happen*. They need knowledge not of the properties of things, but of systems, processes, people, and the relationships *between* things. Businesses are using—and thinking about—knowledge in new ways and this is having a spin-off effect on how knowledge is thought about in the world outside business.

THE NEW WORK ORDER

Fast capitalism's focus on niche markets and innovation has produced a management revolution. Flatter, more devolved management practices are replacing the hierarchical, bureaucratic styles of management of old-style capitalism. A company with a flat management structure has fewer middle managers and even fewer people in the traditional process worker role. Increasingly, the middle-manager role of translating and communicating information from top to bottom is perceived as slowing down a business because it separates its leaders from its products and its customers. If a business is to respond quickly to the needs of its customers, its important decisions need to be made by the people who know most about its products and its customers—that is, those who make and sell the products.

These people need skills that extend well beyond those required of the relatively low-skilled employees of the industrial age business. While these skills encompass those that have until recently been considered workers' skills, they also include management domain skills, and skills that would not have been valued in an industrial-age company. Today's businesses need people who can learn, adapt quickly to new situations, think for themselves, and make decisions. These people have to be able to communicate what they know and what they need to others. They need to work well in teams and take responsibility for completing the parts of a project as well as whole projects—projects that they understand, own, and seek to improve. Their strength lies not in following rules and procedures set by others, but in devising their own systems. These people understand and use technical information (statistics for example), and are adept with complex and constantly changing technologies (computer systems, robots, and so on). They are "systems" or "big picture" thinkers. They—not the top managers—are now an organisation's main problem solvers. They are the company's most important resource, and are critical to its success.

KNOWLEDGE MANAGEMENT IN THE NEW WORK ORDER

Because an organisation's knowledge is no longer the responsibility of a few top-level managers, but of everyone in it, there is now strong interest in developing better systems for organising, managing, and communicating organisational *knowledge*, and for maximising organisational *learning*. The management revolution has produced new branches of management theory that specialise in studying the production, use, and dissemination of knowledge in organisations. In this work, knowledge is something that is produced not by expert individuals, but in *relationships* between the individuals in an organisation. The quality of these relationships (and thus the quality of the knowledge produced) is strongly influenced by the organisation's culture. Similarly, learning is no longer an individual activity, but occurs when an organisation acquires the competencies and skills it needs to be successful. Management theorists say that, from now on, the most successful organisations (and the most successful nations) will be those that are learning organisations, organisations that are able to learn together as a group.

In the new work order, managers are not "bosses", responsible for managing the productivity of the organisation's workers, but "knowledge managers" who are responsible for making sure the organisation's knowledge workers have whatever they need to be innovative. A key part of their work is to foster the kind of interaction—the circulation of ideas, the dialogue between tacit and explicit knowledge, and the translation of knowledge across different expert communities—that produces innovation. Knowledge-management strategies are also important because the new knowledge workers are likely to be contractors brought in to complete specific projects. These highly mobile individuals work for many different organisations, and the knowledge they need for their work is unlikely to become the organisation's knowledge—unless the organisation has a good knowledge-management strategy.

The work identity of these people derives not from who they work for, nor from the kind of work they do, but from the knowledge portfolios they acquire (through their involvement in past projects and/or formal study) and those they plan to acquire in the future. This scenario has some interesting social implications. Because these people are mobile and not connected to any one organisation, they have fewer social connections of the traditional industrial-age kind—workmates, local communities, and family, for example. At the same time, however, they will have a much greater number of other kinds of connections. For example, through the Internet and other communications technologies, they are likely to engage with groups of individuals with similar knowledge portfolios and/or non-work interests, as well as with business contacts and so on. The implications of these new patterns of social connection are not yet clear. For some people, it could mean that their networks comprise only people who are very similar to themselves; for others, it could mean greater diversity of interaction. What is certain, however, is that there will be major changes to community-based forms of social interaction, including those traditionally fostered by schools.

The management revolution outlined above first became evident in the business world, for obvious reasons. However, non-business organisations have followed suit, just as they did in the industrial age, adopting the "new" management practices with enthusiasm. The workplace culture of most organisations is now very different from that of even a decade ago. However, this new work order has, so far, had little impact on the way our education system is organised. The school curriculum, teaching methods, and assessment of student learning are still very much oriented around the needs of industrial age society.

A NEW MEANING FOR KNOWLEDGE?

Many of the academics studying the organisational transformations that are occurring as we move from industrial to post-industrial society think that these transformations have changed knowledge's meaning. In his book *The Rise of the Network Society*, sociologist Manuel Castells says that knowledge is no longer thought of as a "thing", developed and stored in experts, and able to be organised into disciplines. Instead, he thinks people now see knowledge as a form of energy. People treat it as something dynamic or fluid, something that does things or makes things happen. Castells says that, in the organisations he has studied, knowledge is not an object but a series of networks and flows. It is defined not through what it is, but through what it can do. The new knowledge is a process, not a product. It cannot be pinned down or measured, but is always changing. It becomes knowledge only when it is used to produce something new. It is produced not in the minds of individuals but in the interactions between people.

The French philosopher Jean-François Lyotard has also written about knowledge's changing meaning. In a book he wrote in the 1970s, called *The Postmodern Condition*, he predicted that knowledge's importance would derive not from its links with truth, reason, or certainty, but from its "performativity"—its ability to do things. He said that knowledge would become a commodity, something valued according to whether what it produces can be sold, and that anything that could not be digitised would cease to exist as knowledge. According to Lyotard, the traditional idea that acquiring knowledge trains the mind would become obsolete, as would the idea of knowledge as a set of universal truths. Instead, there will be many truths, many knowledges and many forms of reason. As a result, he says the boundaries between the traditional disciplines are dissolving, traditional methods of representing knowledge (books, academic papers, and so on) are becoming less important, and the role of traditional academics or experts is undergoing major change.

All this has obvious implications for education—how it is organised, what is taught, how it is taught, and what its overall purpose is thought to be. Lyotard says that post-modern forms of education will encourage students to learn knowledge derived from the traditional disciplines, not in order to store it away for future use, to reproduce it or add to it, but to do things with it, to remake it in new ways. The "old" forms of knowledge will still be important, but not for their own sake, as they are now. Instead, they will be a resource students will need to generate new knowledge. For Lyotard, the primary purpose of education is to serve the needs of the economy: it is now just a tool for maximising a country's economic performance.

WHAT DOES THIS MEAN FOR NEW ZEALAND?

Much has been written about what countries like New Zealand need to do if they want to be knowledge societies. A report written for the New Zealand government in 2001 by the Science and Innovation Advisory Council is typical of this work. It says that there are four main things we need to work on. First, we need to develop a culture of innovation. Citing the apocryphal Number 8 fencing-wire story, the writers stress that although New Zealanders have always been innovators, we have not always been good at turning inventions into saleable products. We need to develop better connections between innovators and entrepreneurs (generally rather different kinds of people), and to provide better support for innovators through good public-knowledge infrastructures (government, research, and higher education organisations) and transparent regulatory regimes. The second thing we need to do, say the writers, is encourage the development of an effective "cultural mass" made up of knowledge workers who interpret and translate expert knowledge produced in one context for use in another. (This translation and mediation work, some academics argue, is what intellectual work *is* in post-modernism). Third, we need to take account of what the council calls the "triple bottom line", that is, the social, environmental, and economic impacts and benefits of our innovations. Fourth, it says, we need strong investment in ICT, in people, and in education. To be innovative, people need affordable access to information and people. Opportunities for education and training, especially second chance education and specialised training, need to be readily available and affordable—wherever and whenever they are needed.

New Zealand has never been a highly industrialised country. For most of the 20th century, it was reasonably prosperous, with an economy built on the ability to efficiently produce and export agricultural commodities. This period, as we all know, is now over. Britain's entry, in the 1970s, into what was then the European Economic Community, and the resulting huge drop in demand for our agricultural products, forced us to make major changes, many of which should probably have been made much earlier. We can see the influence of knowledge-society ideas in our recent focus on developing added-value agricultural products (instead of, as we did in the past, exporting them in a relatively unprocessed form), and in our focus on customising our products for the needs and preferences of individual customers (a particular restaurant in San Francisco or Tokyo, for example). There has also been huge growth in a range of other service-based industries, such as organised tourism and the export education initiatives. Our government has tried to support the development of new industries in areas of traditional strength. Examples include the food-oriented biotechnologies, our wine industry, and our production of high-value gourmet food items such as truffles, wasabi, salmon, and venison. The government has also tried to develop new partnerships, or "creative synergies", between science- and/or technology-based enterprises and those based on cultural knowledge.

Despite these initiatives, there are, as some commentators point out, no models or templates that we can simply pick up and adopt as a basis for planning our development as a knowledge-based society. Much of the international academic and policy literature on knowledge societies is based on case studies of the development of particular regions (Silicon Valley, for example), which differ in major ways from New Zealand. We need to develop our own local, highly specific responses to the issues and challenges raised by knowledge-society developments elsewhere in the world. There are, of course, many controversial aspects to these developments, and we may decide not to participate in some of them. These issues are beyond the scope of this book, but I would like to look briefly at one of these issues here—the idea of knowledge as something that can be owned—because it has important implications for education.

THE COMMODIFICATION OF KNOWLEDGE, BIOTECHNOLOGY, AND THE IMPLICATIONS FOR EDUCATION

Much of what Lyotard had to say has eventuated. His prediction that knowledge would become a commodity is, as it turns out, a central, and controversial, feature of post-modernism. The capacity to own, buy, and sell knowledge has contributed, in major ways, to the development of the new, knowledge-based societies. Just as an important precursor for the industrial revolution was the "enclosure" into private ownership of land, and later, labour and capital, an important antecedent of the current knowledge revolution was the emergence of the idea of intellectual property. The notion of intellectual property broadens the industrial-age understanding of what a person can own to include ideas and processes as well as things. Someone who has a new idea or who develops a new process can patent it. They can then charge royalties to anyone who later uses that idea or process. Many new developments have become possible because of this shift. One of these, and probably the best known, is biotechnology. A 1930s' legal decision made it possible to patent new varieties of existing plants and animals, and in the 1970s it became possible to patent new, usually genetically modified, life forms. The person who works out a procedure to create a new life form is now entitled to receive royalties on any later use of that process or life form. Individuals or companies now own the rights to sections of DNA, and parts or products of human bodies. These developments are obviously controversial. For some people they are a godsend, a long-awaited new area for economic development that will revive the flagging industrial order. For others, they are deeply morally wrong. They violate the sanctity of the natural order, and interfere with what they see as the essence of what it means to be human. These debates have become familiar to most of us in recent years. But what do they have to do with education?

Some critics of knowledge-society developments say that the extension of ownership rights described above will end the free flow of ideas and knowledge that is supposed to be a key feature of modernism. Knowledge, instead of being a collective good, freely available to all, that is used to develop better ways of living for everyone, will become a private good, available only to those who can pay for it, and used mainly to generate new wealth for the already wealthy. This has obvious implications for education. Publicly funded education is a key part of the modernist project. Through mass education, knowledge is supposed to be freely available to all. An educated population is a public good and is therefore a collective responsibility. Public education is supposed to develop links between the different parts of society and, in so doing, make it possible for everyone to move forward together.

Does this mean that educationists should resist the knowledge-society developments outlined in this chapter? Many people think so. However, for reasons that I hope will become clear later, I argue for a different position. Whether we like it or not, these developments are a reality in the world outside education. They are associated with important social changes and with major changes in the way work is organised and, because of this, we need to respond to them. If our education system is to prepare people to lead productive and fulfilling lives in the world of the future, then, I think we need to rethink much of what we currently do. I am not suggesting that we uncritically accept the business-led vision of the new work order. If, for example, we were to respond to these developments by changing our education system to specifically focus on developing the skills and dispositions needed in the new work order, and *do nothing else*, we would be setting aside the key purpose of a state-funded, mass-education system which is to provide everyone with an equal opportunity to succeed in society. Any move to change this precept would, at a minimum, need to be preceded by extensive public debate.

Some people, of course, argue that reducing the state's role in education is no bad thing. They contend that because education involves getting the skills one needs to get the kind of job one wants, it is an individual benefit, and should be funded by the individual (or their family). I don't support this position, because I think there are good reasons for seeing an educated population as a public good. Public education is one of the few ways a society can try to reduce social disadvantage. If the responsibility for education falls solely on families, existing disparities will simply be replicated, and probably exacerbated, in the next generation. While redesigning our education system to meet the human resource needs of the new knowledge-based society is important, on its own, it is not enough. If we *only* do this, we will exacerbate our current education system's tendency to produce large spreads in educational achievement. The result will be a strongly two-tiered society. One tier will contain a well-educated, highly mobile élite of knowledge workers well equipped to compete in the global marketplace and highly likely to leave New Zealand for better opportunities. The other tier will comprise an under educated, under employed, under class of people who, because their skills, dispositions, and knowledge are not valued in the global marketplace, will probably find themselves excluded from it and, as a result, dependent on New Zealand's social welfare system.

Quite apart from the fact that this is clearly an unproductive use of the country's resources, it would not supply the new economy's human resource needs, and worse, it is deeply unjust. Because it would magnify existing inequalities and breed resentment, it would not contribute to social cohesion and progress. On the other hand, however, if we reject the new capitalism and the new models of knowledge, or simply fail to engage with them, it is highly likely that more and more people will begin to see schools as irrelevant and peripheral to the concerns of the real world. Public education as we now know it will be sidelined and eventually abolished.

I think that we *do* need to respond to these developments, but from a stance that is informed by a critical understanding of where we have come from and where we would like to go. I want to make a case for rethinking our education system in ways that take account not only of knowledge-society ideas, but also of other ideas that are emerging as we move from the modern to the post-modern age. Some post-modern theorists argue that knowledge-society ideas represent the dying throes of modernity. For them, the development of new forms of ownership and the conflation of society and the economy are hyper-modernity—that is, key features of modernity, amplified and taken to their logical conclusion. These theorists say that modernity's preoccupation with knowledge's links with freedom is the other side of the coin that produced the oppression and totalitarianism of the 20th century's major disasters (among them the holocaust and its concentration camps, Hiroshima and Nagasaki, apartheid, and ethnic cleansing). For them, it was inevitable that modernity would turn in on itself and self-destruct.

Other post-modern theorists see the future more optimistically. They say that post-modernism does not represent the end of modernity, or the abandonment of all modernity's ideals. Rather, it involves seeing modernity's key ideas—freedom, equality, justice, knowledge, identity, and so on—not as unassailable givens, but as ideas to be debated, contested, and, where necessary, reformulated. For them, post-modernity involves moving away from trying to achieve absolute ideals. Instead there is a focus on diversity and difference, process, and relationships. Post-modern political activity, moreover, involves a new view of social cohesion. Instead of trying to assimilate all to a standard model, its aim is to allow difference and to find formal ways to include people and things that, in the past, were excluded.

The movement into post-modernity has major implications for education. Public education as we know it is an important modern idea. Education, by developing people's knowledge and their sense of identity, is supposed to be our main means of achieving freedom, equality, and justice. However, because we tend to equate equality with *sameness*, our education systems endeavour to standardise and assimilate—to make everyone the same. This, of course, does not produce equality. The advent of post-modern, knowledge-based societies offers us an important opportunity to rethink our approach to publicly provided education. Part of this process requires an understanding of why our current education system developed in the way it did. This is the focus of the next chapter.

NOTES

Page **24**: Two of the best known of the early sociologists of knowledge are Thomas Kuhn (1970) and Bruno Latour (1987). See also Knorr-Cetina (1981), Latour and Woolgar (1979) and Traweek (1988). For the early sociological work on the development of the information society, see Bell (1973), Toffler (1970), and Touraine (1971).

from the industrial age to the knowledge age

Pages **24–28**: Some general books or articles on the concept of knowledge-based society are as follows: Drucker (1993), Gee, Hull, and Lankshear (1996), Lash and Urry (1994), Neef (1998), OECD (2000), Peters (2001a), Prichard, Hull, Chumer, and Willmott (2000), Stehr (1994), and Thurow (1996). Some of these are written for academic audiences, but others are written for those with business or policy interests. For earlier work on the post-industrial information society, see Bell (1973, 1978), Drucker (1969), Toffler (1970), and Touraine (1971).

fast capitalism, innovation, and change

Pages **28–31**: For three very different accounts of the development of fast capitalism and the new work order, see Drucker (1993), Gee, Hull, and Lankshear (1996), or Harvey (1990). Landes (1998) is a good account of why innovation became such a focus. It also contains a helpful explanation of the development of the new meaning of "quality". For descriptions of the main ideas of the post-industrial age management revolution, see Champy (1995), Drucker (1993), Handy (1989, 1994), Peters (1992), or Senge (1990). See Peters (2001b) for a critical account of these developments. For an account of the changes involved as we move into an increasingly digitised society, including the shift away from thinking in terms of matter or things, to a focus on bits and energy, see Negroponte (1995). Florida (2002) describes the associated revitalisation of some cities, and the rise of what he calls the new "creative class". Harvey (1990) and Jameson (1991) focus on the new consumerism and the new media culture.

knowledge management in the new work order

Page **32**: The new knowledge management systems are described in Prichard, Hull, Chumer, and Willmott (2000), Probst, Raub, and Romhardt (2000), Senge (1990), and Senge et al. (2000).

Pages **33-36**: Carnoy (2000) explores the developments of new forms of work identity that will be a feature of the new economies, and looks at their implications for society in general and for educational policy makers in particular. See also Florida (2002). The cultural changes that we are seeing as we move into post-modernism are discussed in Bauman (1992), Harvey (1990), Jameson (1991), Luke and Luke (2000), and Lyotard (1984).

a new meaning for knowledge?

Page **34**: The ideas on knowledge's new meaning outlined in the chapter can be found in Castells (2000) and Lyotard (1984). See also Gibbons et al. (1994).

Pages **36–37**: The material on what the knowledge society developments mean for New Zealand was derived from government reports and other documents. These include: the *New Zealanders: Innovators to the World* (Science and Innovation Advisory Council, 2001); *Growing an Innovative New Zealand* (Prime Minister's Department, 2002); the Knowledge Wave website (www.knowledgewave.org.nz); *The New Zealand Talent Initiative: Strategies for building a talented nation* (LEK Consulting, 2001); *Knowledge Innovation and Creativity: Designing a knowledge society for a small democratic country* (HUMANZ Knowledge Policy Research Group, 2000); Briefing to the incoming minister (Ministry of Education, 1999, 2002a), *People and Capability* (Ministry of Education, 2001a); *Report of the Compulsory Schools Sector in New*

Zealand (Ministry of Education, 2000); and *The Knowledge Economy* (Information Technology Advisory Group, 1999). For a highly relevant (in hindsight) discussion of the economic issues facing New Zealand as far back as the 1960s, see Sutch (1961). For some recent figures on the large spreads in achievement that are a feature of our education system, see Hattie (2003).

Page **38**: The writers of the report *Knowledge Innovation and Creativity* (HUMANZ Knowledge Policy Research Group, 2000), following Lash and Urry (1994), pointed out that New Zealand will have to develop its own solutions to the issues that knowledge society developments raise for the country.

the commodification of knowledge, biotechnology, and the implications for Education

Pages **38–39**:The term "enclosure" refers to dividing what was previously collectively owned land ("the commons") into smaller parcels that could be individually owned. For a historical account of the social, political and economic changes that were the result of the enclosure movement, see Polanyi (1957), Slater (1968), or Tawney (1912). The 1930s' legal decision referred to in the section on the biotechnology revolution was the Plant Variety Rights Act, and the 1970s decision was the Diamond vs. Chakrabarty case. See Rifkin (1998) or Wilson (2001) for more discussion of these issues. Stewart (1997) outlines the development of the idea of intellectual property.

Page **41**: Beeby (1986) and Renwick (1986) contain very clear statements of the standard social democratic view of public education's purposes, in particular, its links with equality, justice and so on. Gee (2001), Gee, Hull, and Lankshear (1996) and Lankshear, Gee, Knobel, and Searle (1997) discuss some of the issues faced by educationists as we become a knowledge-based society.

Pages **42–43**: The critiques of modernism referred to in the last part of the chapter are taken from Bauman (1989, 1992) and Horkheimer and Adorno (1972), while the "more optimistic" post-modern theorists I refer to are Flax (1990), Yeatman (1994), Yeatman and Wilson (1995), and Young (1990a).

CHAPTER 3

SCHOOLS OF THOUGHT: WHERE DID OUR CURRENT EDUCATION SYSTEM COME FROM?

THE NEW VIEW OF KNOWLEDGE OUTLINED IN CHAPTER 2 is very different from the one on which our education system was built. This is because the new forms of knowledge are a feature of our move into post-industrial society, while our education system is a product of the industrial age. Schools today have many purposes and so draw on many different, often conflicting, ideas. Industrial-age ideas sit alongside other ideas that originated in much earlier times. This chapter looks at some of the key ideas and events that have influenced the development of our present-day education system in order to make the case that many of these ideas need reformulating as we move out of the industrial age.

EARLY IDEAS

Two and a half thousand years ago, Plato designed an education system that was to found his ideal society. This system's curriculum is the basis of what we today call the traditional academic curriculum. While Plato's education system was open to all, its aim was to educate the future rulers of his ideal state. Plato thought that the minds of this élite were best trained by systematically exposing them to humankind's greatest forms of knowledge. This, he thought, would format their minds along the lines of the minds that produced this knowledge. For Plato, developing the qualities needed in a ruler—the ability to pursue truth and justice on behalf of all—required this kind of training. His system aimed to lead students from the empirical world of concrete experiences to the abstract world of pure reason. Education thus meant developing the ability to reason—to use the abstract principles that organise the best human thinking, and the ability to think independently, without reference to outside authorities.

Plato's education system was designed to produce a society that, because it was stable, secure, and just, would bring happiness to everyone. His ideal society had a place for everyone, and everyone knew their place. Plato's education system had open entry, but quickly became highly selective. Only a few received its full benefits—the few who would govern the rest. It was unashamedly elitist, and designed not to produce new knowledge, but to reproduce existing knowledge (and the existing order). Modern Western education systems are directly descended from Plato's model, and, like his system, they are elitist, hierarchical, conservative, and closed.

For two thousand or so years after Plato, formal education in Europe was available to only a tiny fraction of the population. Education was neither universal nor publicly funded. An educated person was one who knew something of the intellectual pursuits of the upper classes. They would have studied languages and literature (especially the Latin and Greek classics), algebra, Euclidean geometry, philosophy, theology, history, and the arts. They were not expected to know anything about the "useful" forms of knowledge—the kind of knowledge that is used to do things or make things. This kind of knowledge was seen as the preserve of the lower classes, and was acquired, not through formal education, but through practical experience gained by working alongside others. Those who acquired a formal education were taught by private tutors, hired by their families, or, later, in England, they may have attended one of the early public schools—Eton, Harrow, Rugby, or Winchester. These schools drew heavily on Plato's ideas. Their main purpose, like his, was to educate the future rulers of society and to reproduce the existing social order.

Plato's model is the basis of the traditional "liberal" education, and its modern equivalent, the academic curriculum. Today's secondary school students continue to study quadratic equations, Shakespeare, Latin, atomic theory, the Krebs Cycle in photosynthesis, Roman history, and a whole host of other things that are not likely to be especially useful to them when they leave school. This is because their teachers (and many of their parents) believe that learning these things will train their minds. Following Plato, they believe that learning these things exposes students to the best and greatest knowledge of their culture, and that this develops their minds in ways that give them access to higher forms of knowledge, élite jobs, and the upper classes.

MASS EDUCATION

The influence of some key ideas and events of the last 300 or so years of European history has meant that modern education systems are, at least in theory, no longer designed solely to educate society's future rulers. While they still aim to develop knowledge and the ability to reason, they are also supposed to socialise the young to fit in to society, *and* to bring out each individual's unique talents and abilities. These last two ideas have their roots in the egalitarianism that is the foundation of public education. Egalitarianism, the philosophy that all individuals are morally equal and have certain basic human rights, is the basis of modern civil society and modern democratic forms of government. It is a philosophy that developed during the Enlightenment, a period of major intellectual and political change that occurred in Western Europe during the 17th and 18th centuries, just before the industrial revolution. Equality and freedom for all were a key part of Enlightenment thought, as was the idea that the purpose of government is to uphold human rights and provide equal opportunity for all.

Mass education was not, however, part of the Enlightenment vision. The idea of having a universal, publicly funded education system as a way of achieving equality and freedom came much later. It wasn't until the late 19th century, in response to the demands of a rapidly industrialising society, that it became common to think that everyone should learn to read, write, and do basic arithmetic, and know something about the world outside their local community. Ironically, mass public education happened not out of a concern for equality and freedom but in response to industrialism's need for an educated workforce. The first state-provided schools were designed not only to teach the basics to everyone but also to inculcate certain habits of mind—respect for authority, piety, reliability, punctuality, and so on. These schools were, of course, primary schools. Secondary education, in most countries, was not the norm until well into the 20th century.

New Zealand established its national system of free primary education with the passing of the 1877 Education Act. Before then, children could attend one of the schools provided by provincial government, or they could go to a church school. There were also some private schools. However, many children, particularly in rural areas, where their labour was important, did not attend school at all, and the quality of the education that was offered was uneven, to say the least. The 1877 Education Act attempted to establish national standards of quality. It also made primary education compulsory for everyone (from ages 7 to 14), and, by making the system secular, it attempted to lessen the influence of the churches on education.

THE GROWTH OF SECONDARY EDUCATION

In 1900, fewer than 10 percent of New Zealand's population went to secondary school. Those who did came from families who could afford to pay the fees (unlike primary education, secondary education was not yet free). Most of those who went to secondary school were headed for university and the professions. In the late 19th and early 20th centuries, New Zealand was a fast-growing colony of Britain. There were plenty of labouring jobs, and for most people, there was little perceived need for academic knowledge or advanced educational qualifications. However, as the country grew, so too did the need for skilled tradespeople and administrators. These people needed an education that went beyond the basics offered by primary school, and so the secondary sector began to grow.

The 1914 Education Act required all state secondary schools to offer free education to all who had passed the Proficiency examination (at the end of the Form 2 year). By 1917, 37 per cent of the population went to secondary school. During the 1920s, the uptake of secondary education increased rapidly. Just as mass primary education came about in order to provide industry with the workers it needed, state-funded secondary education also developed in response to the needs of the economy. However, the early state secondary schools were not well set up for their new clientele. Following the English grammar school system, they offered the traditional academic curriculum. This curriculum, designed to prepare students for university study, was not at all suitable for those with other goals. However, despite more than a century of debate, and several major attempts to reform it, it continues to exert a strong influence on our secondary schools.

One of these reforms was the development, in the early 20th century, of a parallel system of technical high schools that offered a more "practical" and "relevant" curriculum. This idea, in the New Zealand context, was not a success. The presence of these schools allowed the earlier-established academic schools to continue offering the traditional academic curriculum and to continue to scorn practical knowledge. It also allowed the earlier-established schools to position themselves as meeting the educational needs of the professional classes of the future, and to ignore the educational needs of the future plumbers, farmers, bricklayers, and domestic workers. As the headmaster of one of these schools put it, in 1926, his school's role was to "service the professional, official, or business classes" while the local technical school would "cater for the artisan or lower commercial classes". Another principal of the same period voiced the class divisions inherent in this system even more clearly, when she said that, "as a general rule, those who go to the Technical School belong to the labouring classes, while those wanting a 'nicer' education go to the High School." These principals were expressing what many parents believed: if their children went to one of the academic high schools, they were more likely to enter one of the high-status professions and to have a better life.

The two systems, although intended to be equal in status, were clearly differentiated along class lines. The introduction of technical high schools did not increase the value attached to practical knowledge as was intended. Instead, they further increased the status of academic knowledge. The perceived worth of the academic subjects was, of course, completely unrelated to their usefulness as a foundation for life in the professions. Rather, the value of these subjects comes from their historical links with the values and pursuits of the upper classes. Once mass secondary education became the norm, the subjects of the academic curriculum took on a new role. In addition to their role in preparing society's future rulers, they determined who should enter the upper classes. Mathematics, in particular, became the new Latin—the subject that would "train the mind". It was also used to indicate whether a student's mind could be trained and whether it had been trained.

The late 1930s saw another major reform. The unpopularity of the technical high schools forced the government of the day to try a different tack, one that led to the publication, in 1944, of a document known as the Thomas Report. This report set out a new plan for the early years of secondary education, one that was to remain in place for the next 50 years. It introduced School Certificate and abolished the Matriculation examination, replacing it with University Entrance, which could be accredited. However, the key strategy of this report was to establish a new, common, core curriculum designed to provide a "broad and balanced education for all". Material derived from the traditional academic subjects was to be combined with material drawn from the practical subjects, with the aim of providing a secondary system that could cater for students with widely differing abilities, interests, and backgrounds. This new curriculum, compulsory for all students until the end of the fourth form year, was supposed to provide all students, regardless of their background, with an equal opportunity to succeed. However, it was never fully implemented. Schools resisted it by streaming students into different classes based on their ability (as measured by IQ tests on entry to secondary school), and giving these different classes different versions of the core. Although equal opportunity was widely acknowledged as a "useful myth", it officially underpinned all government educational policy for the next 40 years or so.

RECENT DEVELOPMENTS

In the 1980s, New Zealand education had more major reforms. In the early 1980s, the government called for a review of the curriculum. This massive public consultation exercise was to be used to update the school curriculum for late 20th century needs. However, the public's ideas, once collected, were never implemented because this process was overtaken by another quite different set of reforms. Two major reports of the late 1980s, *Administering for Excellence* (the Picot Report) and *Tomorrow's Schools*, marked a major shift in the focus of government policy. The *administration* of education, not the curriculum, was now the central focus. The government replaced the Department of Education with a ministry and made schools into autonomous entities, managed by boards of trustees. Later, in the 1990s, the focus returned to the curriculum. *The New Zealand Curriculum Framework*, with its seven "essential learning areas" (which were not very different from those set out in the Thomas Report's "core") was published. The 1990s also saw a focus on reforming the assessment system, particularly in the upper secondary school, and renewed interest in raising achievement, particularly at the bottom end. Currently, our Ministry of Education's mission is "raising achievement and reducing disparity", and this is to be done via the development and dissemination of "quality" teaching practices that "make a difference".

These reforms have given us a new, more accountable education system, and we are developing new strategies for ensuring that our long tail of underachievers reaches certain basic standards of literacy and numeracy. However, we are ill prepared for the challenges posed by the knowledge society. Our education system's structure, its organising principles, and the assumptions that underlie it are designed to support an industrial age society. For reasons that I outline below, I don't think this system, in its present form, *can* be adapted for the knowledge society. Doing *more* of what we do now, doing it more efficiently, and doing it to a higher standard will not reduce the disparities that are a feature of our current system. This system will not be able to meet the human resource needs of a knowledge-based society, and it very definitely will not offer equality of opportunity. The next section looks at why this is.

THE PRODUCTION LINE MODEL OF EDUCATION (AND WHY IT'S NO LONGER WORKING)

Because our current education system developed to serve industrial age society, it has some important tensions. It is supposed to produce equal opportunity, but, at the same time, it is also supposed to provide the kind of workforce the economy needs. However, industrial age societies are not egalitarian. They are hierarchical, bureaucratic, and highly segmented. If schools are to meet the needs of these societies, they need to be able to turn out two broad classes of people: those suited to working-class jobs, and those more suited to middle-class jobs. Schools are duty-bound not only to ensure that everyone has enough basic education to enable them to find useful employment but also to provide for the educational needs of those destined for professional and/or managerial forms of employment. However, the "extras" of higher education are expensive to provide, and so access to them must be restricted. Thus, schools have to distinguish between those who have the necessary ability (and the work ethic) to benefit from these extras, and those who need only the "basics". In a theoretically egalitarian society, they must be able to do this in a way that is seen as fair, objective, and merit based. In New Zealand, as in most other similar countries, the tension between egalitarianism and the need to meet the economy's human resource needs has been resolved via a structure that combines two key ideas: the industrial age concept of the production line and the (much older) concept of the academic curriculum.

The production line was the industrial age's key innovation. Like the raw materials on a production line, students are organised into batches (or year groups). They progress through a series of steps or stages (known as classes). They follow a curriculum organised as a step-by-step, linear progression from easy to more complex, and which is, apart from a few optional add ons, much the same for everyone. Students receive this standardised curriculum in bite-sized pieces, in a pre-set order. They are taught in groups, using best-practice models of teaching that assume all students learn in much the same way, at much the same pace. Students complete short, segmented tasks that stress speed and neatness over reflection or deep understanding. They are disciplined, and their work is assessed using standardised external quality control checks, that is, they are actively discouraged from developing their own standards of discipline or quality. Their day is divided up into periods of time and units of work, and there is, throughout the system, a strong emphasis on time and schedules, on punctuality and being in the right place at the right time. Like factory workers, they are expected to be respectful of those in authority over them and to conform to the values of the system. They are required to follow instructions accurately and to complete tasks that, because they have usually been broken down, simplified, and separated from their wider contexts, are often quite meaningless to them.

In this model of education, the system's needs are more important than the students' needs. If a student fails to measure up to the system's quality control standards, this is because the student has deficiencies, not the system. Because the aim of the system is to turn out standardised products, it has no way of dealing with non-standard products: they are simply rejected. Similarly, it has no way of dealing with individuals who want to do things differently—who want to experience the system's elements in a different order, for example, or who want to add new elements to the system. Consequently, industrial-age schools produce "bright" kids—those who meet the quality control standards of the system—and "dumb" kids—those who do not. They aim to turn out docile rule followers, people who, in general, accept the authority of others and endeavour to please them. They actively discourage the development of individual authority and intellectual adulthood. They homogenise people and stifle innovation. Their successful students are well prepared to fit in with, and reproduce, the existing systems. Success at school is defined via the education system's quality control checks, known as assessments, the results of which are used to sort students by ability. A high-ability student, that is, a high-quality product, is sent on for further processing, designed to prepare them for professional and / or managerial jobs. Those students deemed to be of lower ability are rejected by the system and allowed to drop off the production line. However, by the time they have been rejected, they will have developed the basic skills and habits needed to work in one of the industrial age's many low-skill jobs. The system is thus a reasonable way of providing everyone with the basics *and* catering for those destined for higher education.

At first glance, this model, characterised by former Director General of Education Bill Renwick as "bread for all and jam for the deserving", seems a sensible way of allocating scarce resources, and, in the industrial-age context, possibly it was. However, this system does *not* produce equal opportunity. It is wasteful, divisive, and in the context of our move into post-industrialism, highly anachronistic. Its supposedly fair quality control system is based on a series of assumptions that, while they have been seriously questioned for generations, persist largely because they are a necessary feature of industrial-age society. One of these assumptions is the concept of ability.

Ability, as all educationists know, is a highly contentious concept. Yet we can't seem to do without it because we need it (or something like it) if we are going to sort people. In our schools, a student has ability if they appear to know a lot about certain kinds of things. If a student has the ability to acquire knowledge of this kind, then they usually (but not always) make good progress in the system and go on to further study. Thus, knowing about some things counts a lot more than knowing about other kinds of things. Knowledge derived from the traditional academic subjects is deemed high-quality knowledge, and students who master it are high-quality students. Mathematics plays a particularly important role here. Mathematics is widely seen as an important subject, perhaps *the* most important subject. Knowledge of mathematics is necessary to progress in the education system, not because of its usefulness in later life (which is, if we are honest, questionable), but because it is widely used to indicate general ability. Mathematics is the prototypical academic subject. It is objective, timeless, universal, and unassailably true knowledge. However, and probably more importantly for the industrial-age educator, it is knowledge that can be organised into a logical sequence of curriculum units that can be taught via expository, step-by-step methods and assessed in ways that produce clear, objective, unambiguous results.

So, just as Plato's system did, today's education system uses the subjects of the traditional academic curriculum for two different purposes: to prepare the future ruling class, and to decide who will enter that class. However, as we have seen, the knowledge that underpins the traditional academic curriculum is the knowledge of the existing ruling classes. Associated with this knowledge are the set of tastes, values, and ways of thinking that belong to that group. The French sociologist Pierre Bourdieu calls these elements "cultural capital". Bourdieu says that each social group has its own, different cultural capital, knowledge that, because it is not taught directly, but picked up through immersion, is not easily accessible to someone from another social group. Schools assume, but do not explicitly teach, the cultural capital of one particular social group, and in so doing, they necessarily disadvantage children who do not come from that social group. Some children from non-dominant groups eventually figure out and adapt to school knowledge (a process that inevitably does a certain amount of damage to their sense of who they are and where they come from). Others simply experience school as alien, and, because they are not successful in it, are damaged in other ways. Bourdieu calls this "symbolic violence" (to distinguish it from actual physical violence), saying that this is how schools play an important role in reproducing the existing social order.

The production-line model of schooling is a one-size-fits-all system. Using the ability to master certain highly specific kinds of knowledge as its quality control mechanism, it sorts people according to their likely occupations in a highly segmented society. It turns out a few people who do very well, a lot who achieve at a reasonable level, and a significant "tail" who do not achieve very much at all. This large spread of achievement, the so-called normal distribution or bell curve, is a *necessary* feature of industrial-age schooling. Our long tail of educational underachievement, recently the focus of attention, is not something new. Although this long tail was routinely acknowledged throughout the 20th century as a problem (and heavily researched by sociologists of education), the problem is one we have yet to solve. We tolerated it largely because there were always plenty of low-skill, reasonably well-paid jobs for our education system's low achievers.

However, as we all know, this is no longer the case. In recent times, New Zealand, along with many other countries, has experienced a period of major economic change. Our economy no longer relies on producing and exporting a small range of agricultural commodities, in relatively unprocessed form. Our focus is now on diversification, on developing new industries and "adding knowledge" to our existing ones. A major consequence of this is that we now have far fewer production-line jobs—producing and processing meat or wool for export, or assembling cars, for example. In most areas of the economy (including farming), there is a strong focus on innovation and adding value, and most jobs now need people who are well educated with good technical skills. We have major skills shortages in some areas, and high unemployment among people with low levels of education.

The government's response to this has been to express concern about the high number of underachievers our education system produces, and to put into place strategies designed to "close the gaps" or "reduce disparities", many of which are specifically targeted at Māori and/or Pasifika peoples. As is well known, our current system is not especially successful in meeting even the most basic educational needs of many Māori and Pasifika students. Māori educators have argued for many years that our education system's Eurocentric one-size-fits-all approach does not connect with many Māori students. It does not allow them to "be" Māori *and* be "educated". However, if current demographic projections are correct, over the next 50 years or so, New Zealand will become a nation of predominantly Māori and Pasifika peoples. If we do not find ways to address the causes of underachievement in our system, there will be a decline in our overall rates of participation in tertiary education and a drop in our average levels of educational attainment. This situation is, of course, more or less the reverse of what is required if we are to successfully participate in the knowledge-based societies of the future. For this reason alone, we cannot continue to have a system of education that aims to produce a standardised product and, in so doing, rejects so many. We can no longer rely on amelioration strategies that focus on doing more of what we do now (or doing it better). Instead, we need to rethink what we are doing, and why we are doing it. In the next chapter, I focus on these considerations, as part of an exploration of how we might escape from the production-line models of knowledge and learning that inform our current education system.

NOTES

Page **47**: Kieran Egan (in Egan, 1997, 2001) gives a very clear account of modern education's multiple purposes and the often strongly contradictory ideas on which they rest.

early ideas

Pages **48–50**: Plato's ideas about education are set out in *The Republic* and *The Laws*. For the standard account of his ideas (and the liberal ideal of education that developed from them), see Hirst (1972). For a critique of Plato's model, in particular, its elitism and its association with closed societies, see Popper (1966).

mass education

Pages **51–56**: For a history of the development of New Zealand's education system, see Harker (1990), McKenzie, Lee, and Lee (1996), Openshaw (1995), Openshaw, Lee and Lee (1993), or Shuker (1987).

For an account of the issues surrounding the development of the technical high schools, see McKenzie (1992). The two principals quoted in this chapter are W. J. Morrell (Rector of Otago Boys' High School) reporting to his board in 1926, and Miss King (Principal of Otago Girls' High School). Their words are taken from the Otago Boys' High School records and are quoted in McKenzie (1992).

The Post-primary School Curriculum: Report of the committee appointed by the Minister of Education in November 1942 (Department of Education, 1944) was known as the Thomas Report after the committee's convenor. The "useful myth" reference is taken from Beeby (1986). Dr C. E. Beeby was the Director of Education in New Zealand from 1938–1960. The other official documents referred to are: *The Curriculum Review: Report of the committee to review the curriculum for schools* (Department of Education, 1985); *Administering For Excellence* (Department of Education, 1988a), widely known as "the Picot Report"; *Tomorrow's Schools: The reform of education administration in New Zealand* (Department of Education, 1988b); and *The New Zealand Curriculum Framework* (Ministry of Education, 1993). "Raising achievement and reducing disparities" is the New Zealand Ministry of Education's current mission statement. See the "about us" section of the ministry's website www.minedu.govt.nz

the production-line model of education

Pages 56–59: For accounts of the industrial-age or production-line model of education, see Beare and Slaughter (1993), Slaughter (1989), Senge et al. (2000), Tyack (1974) and, in particular, Beare (2001). Skilton-Silvester (2003) is an interesting account of a research project that shows how many commonly used teaching practices, particularly those that simplify and break down what is to be learned into discrete tasks, do not develop the abilities needed by the new knowledge workers but quite the reverse: they prepare students for low-status jobs that do not require "thinking between the tasks". Hood (1998) and Pountney (2000) are recent books by two ex-principals of New Zealand secondary school that, in different ways, strongly criticise our current secondary system.

Pages **59–62**: The "bread for all and jam for the deserving" reference is taken from Renwick (1986, p. 26). A large body of work has studied the way the school curriculum is organised hierarchically into high-status and low-status subjects and how this organisation parallels, and reproduces, existing class structures. See, for example, Bernstein (1971), Connell, Ashenden, Kessler, and Dowsett (1982), Goodson (1983, 1988, 1992), Layton (1972, 1995), McCulloch, Jenkins, and Layton (1985), and Young (1971). For material on the role played by mathematics, see Claxton (2004), Davies (1994), McDonald (1992), Teese (1989), and Walkerdine (1988, 1989). Bourdieu's concepts of cultural capital and symbolic violence are outlined in Bourdieu (1971, 1973, 1974). The Italian political theorist Antonio Gramsci makes very similar points in his critique of traditional education (1971). His proposed solution is, however, rather different to the one put forward by Bourdieu. See also Harker (1990) and Nash (1986, 1991).

Pages **62–63**: For some recent figures on our wide spread in educational achievement and the associated "wastage", see Hattie (2003). Bishop and Glynn (1999, 2000), Bishop et al. (2001), Durie (2003), Jenkins and Jones (2000), and Penetito (2002) are a few recent examples of work that argue that it is currently not possible to "live as Māori" and also be "educated" in our mainstream education system. See Cook (2000) or Ministry of Education (2000) for summaries of recent demographic projections.

Page **63**: See Beare (2001), Carnoy (2000), Gee, Hull, and Lankshear (1996) and Senge et al. (2000) for different versions of the argument that the advent of the "new work order" requires everyone to have higher order thinking skills.

Page **63**: Beare (2001) explores some interesting metaphors that we might use to help us rethink education for the knowledge society.

CHAPTER 4

WHERE TO FROM HERE? NEW WAYS OF THINKING ABOUT KNOWLEDGE AND LEARNING

TODAY, EVERYONE, IF THEY ARE TO HAVE A JOB, NEEDS THE kind of higher order thinking skills that only those in managerial or professional positions formerly needed. We can only achieve this through major structural change to our education system. Schools are no longer the main source of knowledge in people's lives. Because we cannot know what we need in the future, it is pointless trying to teach it in advance. The world outside education is increasingly valuing the ability to learn—knowing *how* to learn, how to *keep* learning, how to learn *with others*—over the ability to master specific bits of knowledge. Similarly, the ability to see a number of possibilities for solving a problem is becoming more important than knowing the right answer. Schools need to be able to develop these abilities—in everyone. It is especially important, in terms of this country's future, that they are able to develop these abilities in children from less well-educated families. If we, as a country, think it is important to continue to have a public education system that embraces wider social goals, then we need to grapple with these issues.

An important first step, I think, is to abandon the production-line model of education and to look for new metaphors. We need to emphasise multiplicity, diversity, and connectivity, not linearity, uniformity, and autonomy. We need an education system that develops people's ability to connect with one another, work together across their differences, and add value to each other. A post-modern public education system—if there is to be such a thing—will also need new versions of modernism's other key concepts—equality, justice, and identity. Chapter 5 explores how we might go about doing this. First, however, in this chapter, I explore how we might escape from the production-line models of knowledge and learning that inform our current education system. I look at our current mental models of knowledge, mind, and learning, with a view to explaining why they are no longer a helpful basis for knowledge-age thinking.

WHAT ARE MENTAL MODELS?

Mental models are structures we use to scaffold our thinking. They develop in a particular context, and provide a useful shorthand for framing our thinking in that context. Because they are useful, they become part of our everyday thinking. Eventually, we don't recognise them as models, but treat them as if they were simple, common-sense facts. This doesn't really matter as long as the context stays the same. However, when the context changes, we need to remember to change the models as well. If we don't, the models become more and more dysfunctional, and our thinking is constrained rather than helped.

The models that developed as part of the industrial age, production-line approach to education play an important role in current educational thinking and underpin the way we organise our schools. Most of us do not think about or question them: they are just "how things are". These models are so deeply embedded in our thinking that it is very difficult—if not impossible—to think without them. It is certainly hard to change them. But we can begin to do so by bringing them to the surface to look at them. Only then will it be possible to work out which parts of the models are still useful, and which parts need to be changed.

Our mental models of knowledge, mind, and learning

Put simply, the ideas about knowledge, mind, and learning that inform our current educational thinking go something like this:

knowledge

- Knowledge is "stuff".
- It can be stored—in minds, books, or other kinds of databases.
- Knowledge is true, correct, "the facts".
- It is something stable that accumulates slowly over time. New knowledge builds on older knowledge.
- It is built up by people, and people can "have" it: however, it exists objectively, independently of people.
- There are different branches of knowledge (called disciplines or subjects).

- Each discipline has its own way of doing things, and anyone who wants to be an expert in that discipline has to learn these ways of doing things.

minds

- Minds are like containers (filing cabinets or databases): they store knowledge.
- Minds also process knowledge: they take it in, organise it, and represent it.
- Minds are the places where thinking and learning happens.
- Some minds have more capacity than other minds for storing or processing knowledge.
- The mind is located in the brain, but its activities are distinct from the brain's other functions.

learning

- Learning is the process by which knowledge gets stored in minds.
- Learning is an individual activity: it takes place in individual minds.
- Learning is a process that happens in more or less the same way in all individuals.
- Learners of the same age (or stage of development) will be ready for the same kinds of knowledge at the same time, and will absorb it at roughly the same rate.
- Learning is easier if the knowledge to be learned is broken down into parts and introduced as a series of steps, beginning with the easiest or most basic concepts.

These ideas come from industrial-age thinking and the standard modern theories of knowledge. Philosophers of knowledge make a distinction between knowledge and beliefs, opinions, or information. They do this by defining knowledge as a system of justified, true beliefs. This means that, for something to qualify as knowledge, it must be *believed* as true by its knower, it must *be* true, and its knower must be *justified* in believing that it is true. Knowledge is something that people develop and understand. While it can be represented, stored in and retrieved from books and other databases, it is not actually knowledge unless a person understands, believes it, and can justify it as true. For modern thinkers, knowledge is a thing, a product. It is the end-point or outcome of some thinking (or other work). Knowledge is true, the facts, *because* it is developed by following certain rules or procedures. These procedures differ from discipline to discipline. Historical knowledge, for example, is developed differently from scientific knowledge. However, historical knowledge is true for historians, and scientific knowledge is true for scientists. Knowledge developed by following these procedures is objective, value free, and apolitical. It is above political and economic concerns and therefore intrinsically "good". It belongs to—and must be available to—everyone equally. Knowledge is powerful; it is *the* main way of ending oppression and inequity. Because of this, free access to knowledge is incredibly important in modern thought.

Modern education is strongly connected to this last idea. Public education systems, by providing free access to knowledge, are supposed to lay the foundations for a free and just egalitarian society. The modern school curriculum closely follows this model of knowledge. While its influence is particularly clear in the upper secondary school, it also underpins what is taught in primary schools. The school curriculum consists of a selection of subjects, areas of knowledge that come from, and closely follow, a parent discipline in the universities (which is where the disciplines are actually practised). School teachers aim to get their students to understand the facts of their subject in a way that is as close as possible to the way they are understood by the parent discipline's practitioners. Students are also supposed to pick up some knowledge of the procedures (methods) by which the experts (whether historian, literary critic, or physicist) discover, evaluate, and justify "the facts" in that subject. These procedures, however, are rarely taught directly. Understanding of them is supposed to accumulate gradually—through immersion in a discipline and working with its expert practitioners.

In universities, there are strong boundaries—with only the occasional overlap—between the different disciplines, and the higher-status disciplines have stronger boundaries than the lower-status ones. University teaching encourages people to develop expertise in a discipline by becoming part of it. Neophytes learn and gradually accept a discipline's methods. They develop strong allegiances to that discipline and, eventually, if they become an academic, the discipline becomes a key part of their personal identity. To be formally qualified in a discipline is to be part of that discipline (and to see it as part of oneself). Then, and only then (in the university system), is one thought of as being qualified to teach that discipline to others. Having a Master's level qualification traditionally meant that one was qualified to practise that discipline, while having a PhD gave one the right to "profess", that is, to practise and teach one's discipline anywhere. In this way of thinking, moving from neophyte to expert status is a long and highly structured process. By the time people can claim expert status, they will have been thoroughly socialised in, and committed to, their discipline's ways of doing things. Because school subjects are derived from the university disciplines, they generally follow these ideas. School subjects, like their university counterparts, are heavily knowledge centred. There is a strong emphasis on reproducing existing knowledge, and this knowledge is used to draft those who have expert potential from those who don't. Because rule following and getting the right answer are important, there is a standardising effect.

In this schema, knowledge is an object. Developed in the disciplines, it is passed on by people who are experts in those disciplines. Learning involves taking in, or constructing, this object in the mind of the learner, where it is then stored. A good learner is one who can store that knowledge in a form that closely matches the way an expert stores it. The learner's mind is a kind of container that stores all the bits of knowledge it has learned. Knowledgeable people have a large number of bits of knowledge in their minds. As these people become increasingly knowledgeable, their minds become fuller and fuller, until they are like over-stuffed filing cabinets.

This model of knowledge and learning has always been problematic. When, as is often the case, students' understanding of what they have been taught in, for example, their science class doesn't fit with the scientists' understanding, how is this to be explained? Were the students badly taught? Are the students stupid? Is science just too difficult for students of that age? Or could it be that there is something wrong with this model? One problem is that *individual* knowledge and *disciplinary* knowledge are not—and never can be—the same thing. Another is the view of knowledge as an object (set of items) that is constructed in the learner's mind in a way that corresponds as closely as possible with the set of items found in the heads of disciplinary experts. What these items actually are, what we would find if we could look inside the "black box" of knowledge in someone's mind, is not at all clear.

The idea of knowledge as an object is, of course, a metaphor, a mental model that we use to scaffold our thinking. However, it is a metaphor that, while still useful in certain everyday contexts, is no longer helpful in educational thinking. It persists largely because it fits with most people's understanding of knowledge, and because educationists have not come up with a better theory. While this metaphor has long caused problems in education, it is now a serious problem as we attempt to reorient our education system to the needs of the knowledge society. As long we continue to squeeze our educational thinking to fit with this metaphor, it will be impossible for us to accommodate forms of knowledge that cannot be seen as objects. (I think this is the main reason why it has been difficult for people in education to make sense of terms like knowledge work, knowledge creation, the knowledge society, and so on: they are ideas that are incompatible with the knowledge-as-object metaphor.)

The knowledge-as-object, mind-as-container metaphors work reasonably adequately if we think of education's purpose being to encourage students to acquire certain bits of knowledge and certain ways of thinking about them. Once the knowledge is in the container, our job is done. However, the metaphor doesn't work so well when we start thinking about education as helping people learn how to *do* things with that knowledge, how to use that knowledge to generate new knowledge. We are forced to think of knowledge as something that just sits there, like a lump, in the mind, waiting for the day it might be needed. Somehow, the lump must be mobilised and made available for action. It is difficult enough to think about how this might happen in an individual mind: it is next to impossible to imagine it happening in several minds together, or to imagine how we might mobilise the lump to do things.

The first step in moving beyond the current impasse is to recognise that this metaphor frames our thinking. Making the metaphor explicit (as I am trying to do here) will allow us to develop new and different metaphors that will scaffold our thinking in ways that can accommodate other views of knowledge—knowledge as energy or as a system of networks and flows, for example. We will then be able to think about education in new ways, as a knowledge-building or knowledge-creating enterprise, or as an activity that focuses on "doing things with knowledge".

THE NEW MODEL OF EDUCATION

In the world outside education, knowledge's meaning is changing. Here, people are increasingly thinking of knowledge not as a thing, developed and stored in people, but as a kind of energy, something that does things. They are using the word knowledge as a verb, not a noun, as a process rather than a product. Knowing, learning, and doing things with knowledge are now more important than knowledge itself. People are also moving away from the idea of knowledge as a thing in itself, one that is intrinsically good, useful, and powerful. Knowledge is something that is created not in individual people but in the spaces between people. Its value is determined by what it can do in a particular context, and by whether or not what it produces can be sold. Because knowledge can now be owned, bought, and sold, it is not necessarily freely available to all.

If schools are to usefully prepare students for life in the world outside education, then the present focus on encouraging them to master specific bits of knowledge (and assessing them according to whether or not they have mastered them) is no longer appropriate. Instead, the emphasis needs to shift to developing students' capacity for *knowing*—in all kinds of situations with all kinds of people. I want to stress here that this does not mean students no longer need knowledge in the old sense. Such knowledge is still important, but not as an end in itself. It is now a resource to be used in the process of learning how to learn, and learning how to generate new knowledge. Acquiring knowledge will continue to be important, not as a way of training minds to fit with the logic of existing disciplines, but because it is the raw material for knowing.

While the words "learning" and "learners" (as opposed to "teaching" and "students") now appear frequently in educational discussion, the context in which they are talked about is still one that emphasises the learning of particular kinds of knowledge. Learning continues to be seen as the process of storing important bits of knowledge in individual minds, and learners as the people who do that storing. It still involves the *consumption* of existing knowledge, and the acquisition of knowledge as an end in itself. We have yet to refocus our schools so that they see their core activity as building the capacity for knowledge *production*. While knowledge-society schools need to be able to teach people how to learn, and how to acquire existing knowledge, they must also teach people how to do things *with* knowledge, and how to work with others to produce new knowledge.

The shift in emphasis from *knowledge* to *knowing* is important. Knowing is a process, whereas knowledge is a thing. Knowing is a verb. It involves doing things and acting on things. It involves building relationships and connections. Unlike knowledge, it is not something that can be taken in and mastered. It has no end-point, but is always on the way to something, always in process. Emphasising knowing rather than knowledge allows us to reunite academic forms of knowledge with applied (or vocational) knowledge and to escape the intellectual blind alleys curriculum reformers inevitably find themselves in when they assume that these two forms of knowledge are naturally distinct. The distinction also allows us to think about education, particularly what we think it is *for*, in new and different ways, and to think in new ways about thinking, learning, and ability.

NEW MODELS OF THINKING, LEARNING, AND ABILITY

It has long been recognised that most people's thinking does not follow the model of the autonomous isolated "thinking subject" or *cogito* envisaged by Descartes and other Enlightenment thinkers. However, Descartes' model was, until recently, the basis of most formal theories of thinking and learning, and it continues to inform much of what happens in our schools.

Contemporary cognitive scientists do not see thinking and learning as primarily individual activities. Many recent theories of thinking use metaphors derived from computer science. These theories represent thinking and learning as processes that involve making *connections*. They involve the processing of information in connected systems. Some theorists talk about "distributed" learning or "parallel distributed processing", while others use terms like "connectionism", "situated cognition", or "learning communities". In these theories these processes are necessarily social: they happen in contexts involving relationships with people who are important to the learner. For most cognitive scientists, people form their "habits of mind" (or ways of thinking) socially, through the language they speak, the people they associate with, the tools they use and the ideas they are exposed. Most importantly, though, they form their ways of thinking through the connections they make between all of these things. Thinking and learning are thus not objective, independent processes that occur when certain procedures are followed, but activities that depend on many different connections:

between one mind and another (or between minds and other resources), and between new information and existing knowledge and skills. They are strongly context dependent. The particular thinking and learning that occur in any given situation will be the result of an interaction between many different factors—the situation's physical location, the people who are present, the problem to be solved, the tools that are available, and so on. Not only can thinking and learning happen in many different ways, but the end product of thinking and learning—*what* is thought or learned—can take many different forms, and we can't know in advance what form it will take.

Cognitive scientists no longer see the mind as a container, a place, of more or less fixed size, that stores and processes information. Some are also questioning the idea of the mind as something *in* an individual that functions independently of all other minds. For these researchers, the mind is more usefully thought of as a resource, a nodal point in a network that works best when it is connected to other resources. As Steven Pinker explains it, cognitive scientists do not think of the human mind as if it were one single, general-purpose "computer". They see it as a number of different computers working in different but compatible ways simultaneously. (Such ideas are, of course, deeply unsettling to Descartes' idea of the independent thinker and undermine one of modern thought's most basic assumptions—the concept of the individual. If minds aren't in individuals, then what is an individual? I return to this matter in the next chapter.)

Each computer system, because it evolves separately to deal with a different aspect of the world, has a different way of knowing, a different intelligence. These different ways of knowing develop early in life, probably from different networks in the brain. We all have an intuitive physics, an intuitive biology, an intuitive number sense, an intuitive spatial sense, an intuitive psychology, an intuitive economics and an intuitive knowledge of language. The psychologist Howard Gardner identifies eight different ways of knowing, or forms of intelligence. He calls them verbal-linguistic, logical-mathematical, physical-kinaesthetic, visual-spatial, musical, natural-environmental, interpersonal (understanding of other people) and intrapersonal (self-understanding). Thinking involves applying these different ways of knowing in new situations. According to Pinker and Gardner, we all have all of these different intuitions and intelligences, to varying degrees, and if we are to live successfully in today's world, we need to develop them, to bring them to the fore. This, Pinker and Gardner would argue, is what education is for.

But before we can do this, we need to challenge another basic concept, that of ability. Broadly speaking, most people understand ability as being an individual attribute. It is a fixed quantity of "something" that some people have more of than others. As we saw in Chapter 3, ability is a concept that is vital to our current ways of thinking about education. A person with ability—an educated person—is someone whose learning has been directed towards, and who has acquired, highly specific forms kind of knowledge and who has a good understanding of the ways of thinking that produced it. However, their education has not encouraged them to think in new ways, nor has it encouraged them to understand and develop their own particular ways of thinking, learning, and knowing. This is because our current model of education is designed to reproduce existing knowledge and existing social structures. It does this by sorting people, using a model of ability that strongly emphasises two of Gardner's eight intelligences: verbal-linguistic and logical-mathematical. We have based our schools on the assumption that these two forms of intelligence are the only ones that matter. Having ability thus means being good at things that require these two ways of knowing. Contemporary cognitive scientists, however, see ability rather differently. For them, ability is the *capacity* to think and learn. This capacity is highly malleable. It is developed by bringing out or developing a person's basic ways of knowing—that is, through education. Thus, education's purpose is to *develop* ability, not to sort people according to whether or not they already have it.

These new theories of thinking and learning fit well with the new ideas about knowledge outlined in Chapter 2. The world outside education now values the ability to produce new knowledge over the ability to consume old knowledge. The ability to do things with knowledge in a range of different contexts is now more important than the ability to master existing knowledge in highly decontextualised situations. The ability to "think outside the square" is more important than the ability to follow rules, as is the ability to learn, to go on learning, and to help others to learn. Most of us are aware already that high ability, as measured on standard IQ tests, doesn't necessarily equate with "real-world" smartness. We also know that other kinds of intelligence, particularly emotional (interpersonal and intrapersonal), influence an individual's ability to make it in the world outside education. Some cognitive scientists are dubious about Gardner's notion of multiple intelligences, but nonetheless it has helped challenge the idea that ability is a fixed quantity of something we are born with and that it is mainly linguistic and mathematical. Other kinds of ability—intuition, imagination, the ability to reflect, to tolerate uncertainty and not knowing—are proving to be important, and many psychologists no longer see intellect and personality as separate entities.

In the knowledge-based societies of the future it won't be possible for us to know in advance which forms of intuition, knowledge, or intelligence will be most useful. Knowledge-based societies emphasise creativity and innovation. Because innovation, by definition, can come from anywhere, we need to ensure that our education system fosters the development of *all* kinds of intelligence, especially in children's early years. We need diversity, not homogeneity. Later on, perhaps at the secondary level, we might want to ask students, not if they are bright or intelligent, but *how* are they bright or clever. We might want to ask them which of their different intelligences they are interested in developing further, and to encourage the development of niche schools that specialise in developing different talents. We might also want to pay attention to developing students' awareness of their individual interests, strengths, and weaknesses. We might want to develop their ability to assess the abilities of others, not so they can compare them with their own, but so they can see how to use these abilities to complement those of others in a team.

Schools are organised around these ideas and designed to fit with them. These ideas have long been dysfunctional: however they persist because they meet the needs of industrial-age society. Now, as we begin to move away from industrial-age thinking in the world outside education, the opportunity is there to replace them. This will be difficult, but not impossible. The next, and last, section of this chapter outlines some ideas we could use in thinking about how to go about this. These ideas presented are taken from the work of three very different educationists: one writing over 100 years ago; the other two very recently.

KNOWING AND LEARNING IN SCHOOLS

Education as problem solving

Recently, there has been a resurgence of interest in the work of the American educational philosopher John Dewey. Writing in the late 19th and early 20th centuries, a time of enormous social and economic change in the United States, Dewey argued that, because change is a basic feature of modern life, schools should be organised to prepare people for change. They should encourage growth and adaptability, and equip people to deal with real-world situations and problems. In *Democracy and Education*, Dewey argued that knowledge does not comprise the abstract timeless forms Plato envisaged, but is something that people in real world situations construct through what he called "enquiry". Truth, for him, was not some objective entity existing independently of people's pursuit of it. Instead, it was "what works" in the real world of the here and now. Democracy, he argued, requires that all of us (not just an élite few) be active thinkers, and that education develop the ability for active thinking in everyone.

For him, people become active thinkers through interaction—with other people, with their environment, and with existing knowledge—not by being apprenticed to disciplinary knowledge. Schools should promote activities for the mind and the body: they should provide what he called "organised, purposeful experiences" that emphasise experimentation and communication. In *Experience and Education*, he outlined his concept of experience as a five-step process involving students in:

- having an experience (in which they are genuinely interested);
- conceptualising a problem based on this experience;
- getting information and making observations relevant to the problem;
- developing solutions in an orderly pattern; and
- testing those solutions, not in terms of whether or not they are the "truth", but in terms of which work best and/or are the best available at the time.

The teacher's task is to organise their students' experiences so that they lead to useful problem setting and problem solving, for example, through the setting of open-ended projects or tasks. In Dewey's view, education should be a set of integrating, unifying experiences. It should aim to break down or integrate divisions in knowledge, not encourage their development. For him, there was no division between the academic and the practical, no hierarchy of subjects. All learning, he argued, involves problem solving, whether the problem involves ideas and argumentation, or physical skills and techniques. All learning involves the learner in constructing their own particular knowledge of something through a process of active enquiry, usually in interaction with others, but possibly through reading a book.

Like other 20th century philosophers of education, Dewey's aim was to develop intellectual autonomy and deep understanding, but his means of doing this was very different from the standard 20th century position, as developed by philosophers like Peters and Hirst. Dewey saw intellectual independence and understanding as being developed through structured—or, as we might say today, scaffolded—real-world experiences that take place in a social context. Learning and problem solving, he said, are not activities that take place in the minds of isolated, autonomous individuals, but, as he put it, "in community", in interaction with others.

In his time (and since), Dewey was accused of being anti-intellectual, of undermining the role of the teacher (as the source of knowledge and modeller of expert practice), of emphasising method over content, and of relativism, in the sense that he disputed the existence of absolute, objective truths. Such accusations arise from a commitment to the traditional Platonic model of education. Dewey, unlike Plato, did not think of knowledge as something that is mind expanding in and of itself. For him, it was something developed if and when it is needed to solve a particular problem. The activity of problem solving is what expands the mind, not the acquiring and storing away of existing knowledge. Although Dewey's ideas have been reasonably influential in primary education, the secondary and tertiary sectors have never really embraced them. His ideas about knowledge and education's purpose are very different from the ideas that gave us the traditional academic curriculum: however, they are ideas that can accommodate change and encourage innovation. They can be applied in a wide range of situations and for a wide range of people. They also fit well with the new ideas about knowledge outlined in Chapter 2.

Schools as learning gyms

Dewey's focus was knowledge. A hundred years later, educators dealing with very similar questions are more likely to focus on learning. The British educationist Guy Claxton has developed a concept that he calls "learning power". He proposes that we replace the industrial age factory model of the school with a metaphor that sees minds as bodies and schools as gymnasia, in that their aim is to develop "fitter" minds.

Using this metaphor, we can see minds as entities that, although many shapes and sizes, can all become fitter. They are not just empty vessels to be filled, but are expandable and able to be developed. Being mentally fit, like being physically fit, is a good thing. It allows people to aim for and achieve many other goals. Fitness trainers have a model, based in physiology, of what fitness is, and how it best achieved. Educators, too, have models, from cognitive science, of what mental fitness, or learning power, is, and how it is best achieved. Getting mentally fit requires a variety of mental exercises. If we simply do the same kind of exercise day after day, we will over develop some of our mental muscles and leave others under developed. Getting fit also requires us to stretch our mental capacity, to push ourselves to our limits. The amount of exercise required in this regard will differ for different people in different contexts. Just as gyms have different pieces of equipment designed to exercise the body in different ways, schools need equipment for exercising the mind. Students need interesting and challenging things to work on in relation to the traditional topics, problems, and subject matter. The material used should be chosen for its usefulness in developing a particular aspect of mental fitness, not for its intrinsic worth or its usefulness in assessing mental ability. People don't go to gyms to study the equipment—how it was made, or the names of its parts. They go to use it. Similarly, Claxton argues, the traditional subject matter should be used in schools to develop students' learning power, not studied as an end in itself.

In developing their mental fitness, students will sometimes need help to use the equipment. They will need programmes designed to develop their learning power. These programmes should be of sufficient difficulty to stretch their minds, but not so hard that they give up or are injured. Their "learning coaches", because they are more experienced in the use of the equipment, can help them develop suitable programmes, but the coach's goal always will be to have the students, in time, develop their own training programmes. The equipment—the topics and activities—needs to be designed to suit a range of different starting levels. However, starting level is not ability: the level a person starts at has nothing to do with how far they can go. Learning coaches help students think about and take responsibility for determining the starting point that will best develop their learning power.

While the learning coach's job is to support students to achieve their goals, the students have the primary responsibility for whether or not they put in the work. The learning coach can help students set realistic goals and monitor their progress. They can suggest activities that will help narrow the gap between current and target performance, and they can provide precise feedback on specific aspects of the work involved in reaching the target performance. Learning coaches, like students, are also learners. They, too, are trying to increase their mental fitness. Learning coaches are not expert in everything their students need to know, but are happy to work out how to do something with their students. Part of their job is to model the confidence, openness, and even pleasure in the face of uncertainty that students need to be good learners.

Getting—and staying—mentally fit, like physical fitness, requires sustained commitment. Learners develop mental fitness not by following slick formulae or slogans, but by following sustained programmes that slowly but surely push out the limits of their stamina and strength. The key performance indicator is an increase in each student's personal best, not his or her achievements relative to others. However, as long as the focus remains on improving the personal best, a little bit of competition is a helpful way of increasing motivation for training. Likewise, being in a team, where everyone is trying to get fitter, is also helpful.

Claxton's learning gym metaphor is instructive because it shows us that focusing our attention on learning (the verb) rather than knowledge (the noun) frees our thinking from the old constraints. Straight away we start having new and different ideas about what good teaching involves, what assessment should involve, and what schools are for.

Knowing in teams: Schools as research sites

The American educator Carl Bereiter takes Claxton's idea further. He thinks that schools of the future should be knowledge-creating organisations. For him, the most promising way to start this process is to restructure all school activities so that they resemble the workings of research groups. He cautions, however, that what takes place in these activities must be *real* research. It must be research that investigates real questions and contributes to real progress on those questions. Students must set their own questions, and the questions must be ones that they are genuinely interested in, and curious about, the answers. Like all research in multi-disciplinary teams, this research would take place in groups. The groups will need processes for deciding what questions to investigate, how to investigate them, who will do what, and what the research will be used for. Because each group member will bring a different point of view and a different way of thinking to the group, it will be important to ensure that all points of view are properly articulated and considered, and all group members are genuinely able to participate.

Many teachers will respond to this by saying, "But we already do this." Certainly, there is nothing new in students working together on projects, investigations, or activities that involve "discovery learning". Such activities have been part of most teachers' repertoires for a very long time. However, Bereiter's concept of real research is fundamentally different. He would say that the standard school project or investigation is not research because it is underpinned by the mind-as-container, knowledge-as-object metaphor. Inevitably, he says, this type of activity becomes co-operative learning wherein students help one another learn. While, as he says, there is nothing wrong with this, it does not involve the kind of collaborative knowledge building that students need to be proficient at if they are to contribute to the new knowledge-based societies. When we think using the mind-as-container, knowledge-as-object metaphor, we cannot see the distinction between knowledge creating and learning, so we reduce knowledge building to learning.

Knowledge building, in the sense Bereiter uses it, is a process of generating genuinely new knowledge. It is not learning already existing knowledge but a process that necessarily takes place in groups. The new knowledge comes not out of the minds of individual group members, but from the relationships between them. In contrast, learning, when framed by the mind-as-container, knowledge-as-object metaphor, is the process by which existing knowledge gets "put into" individual minds.

Bereiter's real-research idea involves something bigger than the learning individual students might do. He sees their collaborative knowledge-building efforts as contributing not just to their own learning (although of course it will do this), but to world knowledge—or at least to the collective knowledge of the groups of which they are a part. As he points out, research is not learning (although the individuals involved in a research project will often do some learning), but a process that aims to advance world knowledge. Learning advances only an individual's knowledge. Research is not only more than learning, it is also more than its outputs—the books, papers, performances, and media products that may result from it.

Essentially, Bereiter thinks that we need to start thinking about education as a process of helping people learn how to do things with knowledge in collaborative teams, and how to be knowledgeable in ways that go beyond simply acquiring bits of knowledge. We need to see understanding not as mastering or taking in something, not getting the right answer, but as a process of developing relationships with whatever is to be understood. We need to pay attention to processes and relationships. We need to attend to the spaces between objects and individuals rather than to the objects and individuals themselves. However, the first and most important step in all this is to acknowledge the extent to which the mind-as-container, knowledge-as-object metaphor has influenced our thinking. Only when we have done this will we be able to stop taking it literally, and start looking for ways around it.

ARE THESE IDEAS ENOUGH?

In the conclusion to his book, Bereiter says that, if the knowledge age is to be a good age for humanity, it will be important that schools lead the necessary social change, not follow in its wake. If schools were to respond to knowledge-age ideas by reconstructing themselves as if they were knowledge-creating companies, this would be, he argues, a mistake. Knowledge creation in schools should involve students creating knowledge for their own use, not for sale. Unlike the employees in a knowledge-creating company, students are not selected for their skills: they belong because of where they live. Because schools are more like miniature societies than miniature enterprises, they are, Bereiter thinks, best thought of as little models of the knowledge society, not little knowledge-creating enterprises.

Bereiter thinks we should see the schools of the future as "laboratories for testing designs for the Knowledge Age". If we want the schools and societies of the future to be humane and just places for all, then everyone needs a part to play, and everyone needs to find their part meaningful and rewarding. The knowledge produced must be good knowledge. It must be effective in producing more knowledge, and it must be knowledge that students will want to take with them when they leave school. While schools will obviously face a number of problems as they attempt to do these things, these problems are ones that society as a whole has to solve. Schools are not companies. They are the building blocks of our future society. Moreover, giving people the knowledge and skills they need to get a job is not their only purpose. They are also supposed to lay the foundations on which we can build the kind of society we want. In particular, they are supposed to play a role in building social cohesion. Schools do this in a number of ways. They formally teach people about the society they live in. They try to ensure that people have contact with, and some understanding of, people from different social backgrounds. And they try to give everyone the skills and resources they need if they are to have a reasonable chance of making it in society.

If adopted, Bereiter's real-research model, and the new models of knowledge, mind, and learning that support it, would go a long way towards developing the kind of well-educated, non-standardised knowledge workers needed by post-industrial-age economies. However, on its own, Bereiter's model is not enough to support the development of a public education system that can meet all the needs of a post-modern society. While it will probably be able to build employability, by itself it will not build social cohesion. If we are to continue to have a public education system in the post-modern era, educationists will have to understand and use the new ideas about knowledge. However they will also need to understand and use the new ideas about individuality, identity, and equality. The next chapter looks at these ideas and their implications for education.

NOTES

what are mental models?

Page ***68***: The idea of mental models as providing a framework or scaffolding for our thinking comes from Wittgenstein (1969). This scaffolding is usually a metaphor of some kind. See Lakoff (1987), Lakoff and Johnson, (1980). However, as Lakoff et al. note, when people forget that these metaphors are not real or the facts, the metaphors can limit our thinking and eventually become dangerous.

our mental models of knowledge, mind, and learning

Pages ***69–71***: The philosophical model of knowledge outlined here is the standard definition as used in the modern Western European analytic tradition of philosophy. Accounts of it can be found in any introductory philosophy text, but the references I used were

Anchor (1967), Cassirer (1955), Musgrave (1993), Scheffler (1965), and Seidman (1983).

Pages ***71–75***: See Hirst (1972, 1974) and Hirst and Peters (1970) for the standard philosophical account of the development of school subjects from generic forms of knowledge. However, it is important to note that the forms of knowledge that are the basis of school subjects were, until the 1970s, largely taken for granted. See Hirst, (1974), Hirst and Peters, (1970). The idea that the school curriculum represents a *selection* from available knowledge, made through conscious and unconscious choices by particular people, at particular times, for particular purposes, first appeared in the work of the "new" sociologists of education in the 1970s. See, especially, the collection of papers in Young (1971), and the typology of school "knowledge codes" formulated by Bernstein in his article "On the classification and framing of educational knowledge" (Bernstein, 1971), and later developed in his other work (Bernstein 1977, 1990, 1996). This work drew out the distinction between school knowledge and non-school (or real world, common-sense) knowledge, and between high status, academic forms of school knowledge and low status, practical forms. It argued that breaking down the distinction between the two would be an important catalyst for social change. Later work has explored the processes that new school subjects go though if they are to be high status subjects. See Goodson's (1983) account of the contrasting development of geography and environmental education or rural studies as school subjects. Other work explores the different developmental pathways of design/ technology, horticulture, media studies and computer studies. See Goodson, (1985), Layton, (1995), McCulloch, Jenkins and Layton, (1985), Paechter, (2000).

the new model of education

Pages ***76–77***: A recent report by the Knowledge Policy Research Group of the Humanities Society of New Zealand (HUMANZ, 2000) points out that the advent of knowledge-based societies does not mean that the old disciplines no longer matter. Indeed, as it argues, the provision of public access to old knowledge is a necessary pre-condition for a democratic society. For an account of cognitive science's extension of the philosophical idea of knowledge to include beliefs, know-how, and so on, see Anderson (1983).

new models of thinking, learning, and ability

Pages *78–79*: The cogito or "thinking subject" envisaged by Descartes in his famous phrase *cogito ergo sum* (I think, therefore I am) was an entirely autonomous being whose thoughts were entirely his own, developed in isolation from all other thinking beings. The ability to engage in this kind of pure, abstract rationality was, for Descartes, what distinguished humans from the animals. The ability to think in this way meant that one was aware of one's own existence, and was, therefore, a thinking, sentient being. In contrast, the philosopher Ludwig Wittgenstein (1972) argues that it is impossible for an individual's thinking to be isolated from that of others. We are born into language, we are part of it, and we cannot think without it. Because language is public and social, we are not capable of private or pure thoughts uncontaminated by the thoughts of others. For Wittgenstein, language comes before—and constructs—the *cogito* or thinking subject. The thinking subject's thinking—and therefore his or her world—are made possible *and* limited by language. The educational psychologist Lev Vygotsky makes a similar argument from an educational perspective in his book *Thought and Language* (1986). For him, all knowledge and thought is socially constructed in language in various "zones of proximal development", that is, in the presence of various significant and more experienced others.

Pages *79–82*: Distributed learning, situated cognition, and learning communities are now widely used terms. They refer to a non-individual model of learning, in which learning is seen as a highly complex activity that is situated in and distributed, or stretched, across different minds, bodies, activities, tools, and culturally organised settings. These terms first appeared in the work of Brown and Palincsar (1989), Lave (1988), Rogoff (1990), and Rogoff and Lave (1984), but see also Bereiter (1994), Bereiter and Scardamalia (1993), Brown, Collins and Duguid (1989), Brown, Rutherford, Nakagawa, Gordon, and Campione (1993), Lave and Wenger (1991), Lea and Nicoll (2002), and Salomon (1993).

For an account of the parallel distributed processing model of learning (PDP) and connectionism, see Rumelhart (1989) and Rumelhart, McClelland, and the PDP Research Group (1986). These learning theories are now commonly applied to societies and organisations, as well as to individuals. A learning society or learning organisation is thus one that has extensive networks and interactions across different knowledges, communities of practice and organisations and social contexts. For the cluster matrix theorists (see, for example, Brown and Duguid, 2000), learning takes place best where many ideas are circulating, and where there is extensive cycling between tacit and explicit knowledges.

For accounts of contemporary cognitive science's view of thinking, see Gardner (1985, 1991), Hirschfeld and Gelman (1994), and Pinker (1997, 2002). See Gardner (1983) for the early account of his idea of multiple intelligences, and Gardner (1999) for the later, updated version. According to Pinker (2002), one of the main purposes of modern education systems is to overlay—or, in some cases, to counter—intuitive ways of knowing with the more advanced forms of knowledge that people have developed in the relatively short (in evolutionary terms) period of human existence that has involved a settled, "civilised" way of life.

For critiques of the old idea of ability as a fixed, measurable quantity of something that some people have more of than others, see Gould (1981), Herrnstein and Murray (1994), Jacoby and Glauberman (1995), McDonald (1998), and Olssen (1988). Many leading New Zealand educators have, for years, railed against the influence this concept has had on schools, particularly our secondary schools. Some have put forward detailed proposals for reform. See, for example, Hood, (1998), Pountney, (2000).

For explanations of the role of emotional or interpersonal and intrapersonal forms of intelligence, see Goleman (1996) or Sternberg (1996).

Chiu, Hong, and Dweck (1994) outline recent work that signals the breaking down of the traditional distinction (in psychology) between intellect and personality.

knowledge and learning in schools

Education as problem solving

Pages ***83–86***: Dewey's idea on the purpose of education and his problem-posing model of education are taken from his books *Experience and Education* (1938) and *Democracy and Education* (1963).

Schools as learning gyms

Pages ***86–88***: Guy Claxton's "gymnasium" model of schooling and his "learning power" idea are outlined in his books *Wise Up* (1999) and *Building Learning Power* (2002), and also in a recent paper (Claxton, 2004). *Building Learning Power* has many practical tips for teachers.

Knowing in teams: Schools as research sites

Pages ***89–91***: Bereiter's idea of school as sites for research comes from his book *Education and Mind in the Knowledge Age* (2002). The idea of reconfiguring all school activities as research is outlined on p. 21, and the reference to schools as models for the knowledge society p. 92—as "laboratories for testing designs for the Knowledge Age"—is on p. 462 of his book.

CHAPTER 5

RENEWING SOCIAL DEMOCRACY: BEING EQUAL *AND* DIFFERENT

AS WE HAVE SEEN, OUR EDUCATION SYSTEM IS FOUNDED on the standard Western view of knowledge. It is also founded on the standard Western view of individuality—or what it means to be a person. Knowledge and individuality are closely connected. If one changes, we can expect to see changes in the other. In this chapter, I argue that our understanding of individuality is changing along with our understanding of knowledge. We need to respond to these changes, not only because they are part of the world today's young people will live in, but, more importantly, because they offer us a framework for thinking our way out of one of public education's most intractable dilemmas—the tension between egalitarianism and excellence.

The chapter begins by outlining the standard model of individuality and how and why it is important in our current education system. It then looks at the new models of individuality and social cohesion proposed by several post-modern political theorists, and explores how we could realise these in our education system. The chapter's key message is that it is no longer appropriate to have an education system premised on a one-size-fits-all model of individuality. For important economic and social reasons, a post-modern education system has to make possible multiple ways of being. However, this does not mean that anything goes and/or that nothing matters.

THE CURRENT CONTEXT

Recent government policy documents have routinely presented education as the solution to the problems we face as we try to become a knowledge society. Education, we are told, is a critical factor in our goal of achieving stronger economic growth. We need to invest in a "quality" education system to "grow our pool" of the "exceptionally talented", while at the same time also "raising everyone's game". Education is thus supposed to provide the resources we need for economic growth. At the same time, however, it is meant to build social cohesion—the sense of society or inclusion we need if we are not simply to export our talent.

This is asking a lot of an education system designed for industrial age needs. As we saw in Chapter 3, our current system, because it is based on industrial-age thinking, is not good at dealing with difference, and it produces a great deal of waste. It is not good at meeting the needs of the exceptionally talented, nor is it well set up to improve matters for its underachievers. The approaches to knowledge it emphasises are not a good basis for developing the kind of knowledge workers we will need in the future.

We can increase our investment in improving the existing system's quality all we like, but this will not produce the kind of changes needed for a successful knowledge-age system. Among the major changes that we need to make are those that relate to two key ideas: equality and knowledge. Both of these ideas are very important to our current education system. If we wish to retain a public education system, they must continue to be important. However, because of their history, and other ideas that go with them, these ideas, in their current form, do not work very well as the basis of a knowledge-age education system.

EQUALITY AND EDUCATION

Like all industrial-age education systems, the New Zealand system is, at least in theory, structured by the principle of equality of opportunity. The 1877 Education Act established a national system of free compulsory primary education for all children. This system was designed to standardise the quality of education offered around the country (which had been very uneven), to reduce the influence of the churches, and to provide every child with the foundations they needed if they were to have an equal opportunity to succeed in life. But over time we have taken equality to mean sameness, and in so doing have developed a system that does not give people equal opportunity but turns them out to fit the highly segmented industrial-age workforce. Moreover, because higher education (until recently) has been a scarce resource that is rationed to those with the necessary ability, our secondary schools are hierarchical and competitive. They are designed to weed out those who don't have what it takes for higher education.

This has long been a problem. However, as we move into the Knowledge Age, it is a problem that is becoming more pressing. Equality is—and must continue to be—a key goal of any public education system. However, the modern idea of equality is now being strongly challenged. We need new ways of thinking about equality, ways that do not involve sameness, or one-size-fits-all approaches. The first part of this chapter looks at how our mental model of education is influenced by our understanding of equality. Later we look at how and why this is no longer appropriate in today's context.

OUR MENTAL MODEL OF EDUCATION

Like our ideas about knowledge, current ideas about education are primarily industrial-age ideas. Put simply, they go something like this:

- Education is "a good thing", and the more of it a person has the better.
- Education helps people to fit in to society. It builds understanding between different groups and so is an important part of the "glue" that holds society together.
- Education, if a person makes the most of it, gives that person the opportunity to succeed in life. It is an important way of equalising people's life chances.
- Success in education is a combination of ability and effort. If you have ability and work hard, you will succeed. However, some people will naturally be more successful in the education system than other people because they

have more ability and work harder. This is how it is in the real world, and so this is how it should be in the education system.

- Education is socially neutral. It treats everyone equally, and that is how it should be in a just society.

However, all the evidence on school outcomes tells us that schools generally do not make a great deal of difference to people's life chances. Schools are not neutral, and many people's experience of the education system is not a good one. Why is this? Is there something wrong with those students who aren't able to use the education system to improve their life chances? Or is there something wrong with the schools these students are in? Are these schools doing the wrong thing, or are they perhaps not trying hard enough? Could they do more? Alternatively, does the problem lie with society? If schools are part of a society that allows poverty, poor health, and so on to be inextricably linked with educational underachievement, is it fair to expect schools to overcome the effects of these things on their own? Given that our thinking is framed by the assumptions listed above, these three positions are all that is available to us as we try to work out why our model of education doesn't produce the outcomes it is supposed to.

Various educators (and bodies of educational research) support each of the three positions (see the notes at the end of the chapter for more details), and all three have some truth. Schools on their own cannot overcome all the effects of low income, poor health, sub-standard housing, and so on, and some students don't seem to be able to take in the kinds of knowledge that schools offer. However, accepting that we can't do very much with kids from poor areas is to pose the question of why we have schools in the first place. If we know that children from these backgrounds are unlikely to succeed, and we don't think there's much we can do about it, then why do we continue to require them to attend school?

Instead of continuing to debate the relative merits of these three positions, I think we need to move away from asking why some students succeed in the education system while others don't, and what it is that schools, society, or individual students do wrong, to asking how the disadvantage of some students relative to others is *produced* by our meaning system. How is that we come to believe that some students' lack of success is just "how things are"? To answer questions like these, we need to look very carefully at the assumptions that underlie each of the three positions outlined above. We need to dig below the surface of these assumptions, to see what drives them, and to decide what, if anything, of what we find we should keep as we try to develop a new model of education.

WHERE DOES OUR MENTAL MODEL OF EDUCATION COME FROM?

Our mental model of education is informed by two closely related philosophies: egalitarianism and individualism. These two philosophies are a very important part of modern Western industrial-age thought. They are the basis of all modern political and economic theory, and all the social institutions, including education, that have developed from these theories. Underpinning these philosophies are a number of assumptions, which are as follows:

- People are individuals.
- They are self-contained beings, separate from all other individuals, both in bodily terms, and in terms of their thinking processes.
- They should be completely free to choose how to live their lives (as long as their choices don't interfere with the freedom of others).
- All individuals have certain basic human rights. They must all be equally able, and free, to participate in public life. If, for some reason they are not, it is the political system's responsibility to intervene to make sure that they are. (This is why we have publicly funded education, health care, and social welfare systems.)
- Knowledge is a set of universal truths that should be publicly available to all. All individuals are equally able, and free, to be the subjects or knowers of this knowledge.

These ideas probably seem self-evident, and that's hardly surprising, given that they are the basis of modern thought. However, there is now a substantial body of work (by post-modern political theorists) that argues that these ideas are not self-evident, and, furthermore, that they are based on a number of important omissions.

SO WHAT'S MISSING?

Twenty years of work by feminist scholars has shown that, in Western European thought, all individuals are people, but not all people are individuals. Several major groups of people are not—and have never been—included in the modern Western concept of individuality. When this concept first developed, the individual was an independent head of household who governed those who came under (typically) his household's jurisdiction as its dependants. Within this system, known as patrimonial democracy, it was legitimate for adults who could not establish their own households to depend on those who could.

The household was thus the main political unit, and the head-of-household was the main political actor. The head-of-household "stood for" the other people in the household and, in political terms, he effectively *was* the individual. The other household members, because they came under his protection and jurisdiction, were deemed part of him. The individual of modern politics was therefore a white male property-owning person. Women, children and servants were very clearly not individuals. These people, if considered at all in early liberal political theory, were part of the domestic sphere. They did not participate in the political, economic, and intellectual activities that are the basis of public life, but, importantly for later developments, they were not *conceptually* part of it. These people were not seen as autonomous independent thinkers, and they were not free to live their lives as they chose. They did not have equal access to knowledge, and, because they were not rational, they could not be the subjects, or creators, of knowledge. They were not equal, they did not vote, and they did not have the same human rights as those who were individuals. Accordingly, modern Western thought's two key philosophies—egalitarianism and individualism—when first developed, excluded women and other non-property-owning people (the working classes, for example). They also did not include the indigenous peoples of the countries that were later colonised by Western European powers.

This way of thinking is, of course, no longer legitimate. It has been destabilised by generations of activism on behalf of women, working-class people, indigenous people, and disabled people. These people are now formally included in this model of individuality. In theory, they have equal rights. They can vote, own property, and demand redress if treated unjustly. However, because of the way it originated, this idea of individuality still has serious problems. One of these problems, one that has implications for our model of public education, has to do with the logic of equality. Social justice, in the modern political system, depends on the concept of equality. When it can be shown that a person or group has not had an equal opportunity to succeed in society, this is an injustice, and, for the system to be legitimate, it must be rectified. However, because equality is taken to mean sameness, if the person or group is to prove that they have been treated unjustly, they must show that they are the same as everyone else.

This requirement is, not surprisingly, fraught with problems. The early feminists, for example, had to argue that women were the same as men and should therefore have equal rights with men. While this argument eventually achieved formal equality, it doesn't work that well in practice. Women and men are not actually the same. They have different experiences and are treated differently. However, because we don't have the conceptual tools for thinking about people who don't fit with the one-size-fits-all model of individuality that we have—the white, middle-class male model—differences can only be seen as defects, as having something mising. Equality *with difference* is thus not possible within this model. Other previously excluded groups, as they have argued for formal equality, have had similar experiences. They too have been positioned as deficient, as not having what it takes. These groups, while formally having equal rights, because they are not *the same*, actually are not recognised as being genuinely equal.

In response to this situation, political activism on behalf of excluded groups began, in the late 20th century, to take new forms. Liberal activists became radicals. They stopped claiming equal rights and sameness, and started arguing that the groups they represented were different from—and better than—the "standard" individual that is the reference point of modern political thought. The result of this was the proliferation of a whole range of new and different identity categories—women, Māori, gay people, disabled people, and so on. These people then had to make their case for inclusion in competition with the representatives of a whole range of other apparently new identity categories. There were arguments about which oppression "came first" or which was the worst. Alliances between these groups weakened, and separatism became the main political strategy. Those who were critical of this approach called it "identity politics" or "essentialism".

This work was important because it made it obvious that the standard one-size-fits-all model of individuality does not fit everyone, but actively excludes a significant proportion of the population. However, it did not solve the problem of how to argue against injustice from a position of difference. It is logically impossible, within modern political thought, to claim equality while at the same time *also* claiming difference. Post-modern political thought developed out of this difficulty. Post-modern political theorists are interested in the concept of difference. They are interested in thinking about it not as the antithesis of equality but as an interdependent term. Emerging out of this work are some interesting new ways of thinking about individuality and identity, and some new ways of thinking about politics and political activism. This work, it seems to me, is highly relevant to educationists.

BEING EQUAL *AND* DIFFERENT

Post-modern political theorists say we should move away from the one-size-fits-all model of individuality and equality. They think we should look for new and different ways of thinking about individuality, ways that allow difference to be expressed *as* difference rather than as deficiency, lack, or exclusion. This approach is known as the "politics of difference" to distinguish it from the "identity politics" it rejects. Post-modern scholars do not say, as some claim, that we should abandon egalitarianism and individualism. Instead, they argue that we can't just reject these ideas because we don't, as yet, have any other ideas with which to replace them. Moreover, these ideas have structured our thinking for so long that it is not easy to think without them. But this doesn't mean that we have to treat these ideas as givens: we can deconstruct them. We can dig up the assumptions that underlie them, have a good look at them, and, where necessary, change bits of them. Some scholars argue that the act of doing this will be sufficient to produce change. They say that simply bringing the assumptions that underlie an idea out into the open will change the way the idea works.

Instead of thinking about egalitarianism and individuality as absolute ideals that can be defined ahead of time and applied to everyone, post-modern political theorists want to think about these concepts as starting points for discussion and debate. They want the focus to be on developing contexts and processes that allow debate and provide space for previously excluded groups to have a voice. Their goal is to find ways to make difference part of the debate, not so that it can be assimilated (or made the same), but so it can just *be*, so it can express itself on its own terms rather than in reference to existing norms. This approach, the post-modernists say, will allow previously excluded groups to work out their own different conception of individuality. What they are seeking here is a rethinking of equality and individuality in ways that allow us to recognise different ways of being and different ways of knowing and learning.

Unlike the identity politics that emerged from the radical feminism and Māori activism of the 1970s and 1980s, post-modern political activism does not aim to create new identity categories. Instead, as one theorist puts it, its aim is "to work difference together", to build relationships that allow the partners to acknowledge and genuinely recognise each other's differences *as* differences, not deficiencies. These theorists reject the modern focus on equality as the ideal, favouring instead an emphasis on plurality, difference, and diversity. Similarly, they want to replace the modern one-size-fits-all concept of individuality with one that emphasises a multiplicity of ways of being. Instead of seeing our identity, or sense of self, as a coherent, enduring set of features that we are either born with or develop (as, for example, a Māori, a woman, or a New Zealander), post-modern theorists see identity as multiple, complex, and constructed. Where the modern individual had *one* stable identity, the post-modern person has to manage many identities in many different contexts. His or her identities shift, overlap, and sometimes contradict one another. Where the modern individual was self-contained and independent, the post-modern person's identities are inseparable from the identities of others. As one writer explains, their selves are "saturated with" the selves of others. Their identities are immersed in, and constructed by, the wider social world. The ideas and practices that circulate in that world determine who a person can be and what it means to be that kind of person. In post-modern writing, these ideas and practices are called discourses, and the ways of being they offer are known as subjectivities.

MANY WAYS OF BEING: DISCOURSES AND SUBJECTIVITIES

Discourses are systems of language, knowledge, social practices, and power. There are many different discourses. Each has different practices, forms of knowledge, and forms of power. Each also has its own language, its own particular ways of talking about things. There are rules for who can speak, what they can say, and how they can say it. These rules are not explicitly taught, but everyone who participates in a discourse knows them, whether consciously or unconsciously. The language used in a given discourse doesn't just describe or represent meaning: it actively *constitutes* it by talking it into place, or bringing it into being. Different discourses offer different ways for people to *be*— or different subjectivities. For post-modern thinkers, the discourses we inhabit form our identities, or subjectivities. Some people think of discourses as being like a series of criss-crossing threads, no single one of which goes right across the whole social fabric. In this analogy, subjectivities are the places where these threads cross over, that is, where discourses intersect. Others think of discourses as being like the lines of force that exist between the two poles of a magnet. Here, the different subjectivities that are available are like iron filings in the magnet's force field: if the force field shifts, the iron filings will rearrange themselves into new positions.

The knowledge society, for example, is a discourse. It is an idea that comes into being through its association with other ideas. It has a history and its own particular language. It is associated with particular forms of knowledge, social practices, and forms of power. It makes certain ways of being possible, and it closes others down. Because key elements of it are said, and repeated, in particular contexts, by particular people, in particular ways, they are "talked into place". They achieve a life of their own and are treated as facts. This talking into place is not, however, just talk: it has real material effects, one of which is that knowledge's meaning is changing.

Another example, that will be familiar to educators, is the discourse of developmental psychology. Developmental psychology underpins the prevailing view of child development as a process of ages and stages. It also underpins the child-centred philosophy of teaching that is *de rigueur* in teacher education. However, some "critical" psychologists say that telling teachers and parents about child development as a series of stages ensures that children do, in fact, go through these stages. Children who don't appear to be following this pattern are put into remedial programmes to correct their development. These theorists argue that children don't "naturally" develop through the standard set of stages: rather, their development is constructed to fit with the framework provided by the discourse of developmental psychology.

All of us participate in many different discourses, often at the same time. We are all able to move easily between different discourses. Our ability to function adequately in each of them depends on our implicit understanding of the rules of the game in each discourse. These rules govern who we are in that context, what we should and should not do, and what will happen if we break them. We develop an ability to function, more or less successfully, in a range of different situations. We also develop the ability to move between different situations and to play different roles in those situations, and to alter the situations we find ourselves in.

These discourses constitute us: they have a major effect on who we are, who we can be, and who other people think we are. When immersed in a particular discourse, we effectively *are* what it is possible for us to be in that context, unless we know enough about how it works to find a way to make it work differently. Because we participate in many discourses, we have not one but many subjectivities. Our subjectivity is therefore not a unified whole but different in different discourses. Because we find some discourses more comfortable than others, we perform some of our subjectivities better than others. However, subjectivity is not just a performance. Who we are and who we can be are materially different in different discourses. While we can emphasise different aspects of ourselves in different contexts, we are also constrained by how we see ourselves—and how others see us—in different contexts. This is especially the case in contexts we are not very familiar with.

Thus, subjectivity is shifting, fragmented, and multiple. The post-modern person is a hybrid—someone who must constantly negotiate boundaries between the different parts of themselves and between themselves and others. There is no one, core, permanent self. According to one theorist, "subjectivity is a complex *verb,* rather than a noun". It is always in process, never finished. One consequence of this, the more psychoanalytically oriented theorists say, is that the post-modern subject does not have to reject or split off unwanted or contradictory parts of themselves. According to another theorist, the *mestiza* identity is pluralistic: it accepts all of its parts—"the good the bad and the ugly . . . the white parts, the male parts, the queer parts, the vulnerable parts". It also accepts all these parts in other people.

DISCOURSE, DECONSTRUCTION, AND CHANGE

Post-modern theorists think that because we are constructed in discourses, and that if we understand these discourses sufficiently, we can construct ourselves differently. Understanding discourses is thus the key to social change. They say that we will not change things by tinkering with the surface features of individual people, groups, or institutions. Instead, we need to play with discourses: we need to change the practices, languages, and knowledges that construct people and things in particular ways. But how do we do this? In endeavouring to answer this question, let's go back to the magnet analogy. If the meaning of each individual iron filing is determined by its position in relation to all the other iron filings in the magnet's force field, then repositioning the magnet (and thus its force field) will give each iron filing a new meaning. If we extend this analogy to society, people are like iron filings: the meaning given to their particular qualities or attributes is constructed in the force field of discourse. If this force field/discourse is realigned, the meaning can be reconstructed. This idea is the basis of the post-modern model of change. If we analyse the terms and conditions of a discourse and look for ways to disrupt or unsettle some of those conditions, we can reposition its lines of force, a process that will allow new meanings and new subjectivities to develop.

This is why post-modern theorists pay considerable attention to analysing discourses. They explore the languages, knowledges, and practices that allow particular discourses to work. They are particularly interested in gaps and points of contradiction—people, ideas, or things that, while they are present and clearly necessary, do not speak and are not spoken about—because exposing these gaps allows us to see and then reposition the discourse's lines of force. Because this process aims to reconstruct unwanted constructions, it is called deconstruction. In Chapter 6 we return to deconstruction. However, you may, by now, be wondering where we are going with all this. Why are we spending so much time on all this esoteric post-modern theory? What does all this have to do with education and the knowledge society?

There are three different—but related—reasons for outlining these ideas here. The first is that while these ideas are currently influential among academics in a wide range of different disciplines, they are not just the products of some ivory tower intellectual game. Nor do they exist only in the heads of a few academics. These ideas represent a serious attempt to understand and respond to real events and trends out there in the world. The second reason is that these ideas offer us a framework for developing new, post-industrial-age versions of individualism and egalitarianism. The third reason, and probably most important one in terms of the goal of this book, is that these ideas give us a way to think about what we could actually *do* in schools to ensure all our students are ready for life in the knowledge society. In the next section, I say a little more about each of these reasons.

IDENTITY IN THE REAL WORLD

In the everyday world, the old one-size-fits-all model of individuality was replaced long ago. Consciously or unconsciously, most of us know that we have multiple identities, that these are fragmented and shifting, and that they come into being though our connections with others. This view of identity is well established in the media and in popular culture. Advertising no longer targets the standard demographic segments—adolescents, retired people, or housewives, for example. It is customised for the needs and preferences of small, highly specific, niche markets. Diverse lifestyles and diverse needs and preferences are assumed. Consumers express their identity via their product choices—their shoes and their clothes, their preferred drink. The dividing line between the serious media and the tabloids, between information, entertainment, and advertising, is no longer clear. This, according to some commentators, is producing new and more democratic forms of public life.

In the new online forms of communication, the standard model of individuality is long gone. People routinely use Internet communities (chat rooms, online games, and so on) to play with their identity, to construct and reconstruct themselves in ways that have very little to do with their real world, real-time bodies, Many individuals use these spaces to create new, previously unimagined, identities. The development of Web home pages also disrupts the old concept of identity. Home pages represent an individual's—or an organisation's—identity through an assemblage of various pieces of text, images, and sounds that have links to other websites. People construct, or "brand" themselves, via a collection of objects, associations, and connections. This virtual identity is entirely constructed. It is achieved through regularly updated associations and connections. A person's web identity is the images, text fragments, and links to other sites they have chosen to represent themselves. Many people have several web pages. They might have one to represent their work, professional, or business identity, and another to represent their other identities, as, for example, part of a family and/or as a person with special interests or hobbies. The purpose of a website (and, more recently, a weblog) is to create a web identity that will connect the owner to virtual communities of like-minded others.

These developments are highly significant for educationists. The new ICTs and the forms of communication associated with them are an integral part of most young people's lives. Many say they couldn't imagine life without them. Mobile phones and computers are their main means of communication. Their parents and teachers worry about this apparently obsessive communication. Are they getting enough sleep? Can they still spell properly? Will they get OOS? Are their brains developing differently? Does this mean the end of the book? Does it mean the end of the English language, as we presently know it? Because these technologies are strongly associated with youth culture, many people regard their use in educational contexts as inappropriate—harmful even (and it is common to confiscate mobile phones or iPods that are used in class time).

But these technologies are part of something much bigger—something that we cannot ignore. This something bigger, this zeitgeist or paradigm shift, involves the developments that are the subject of this book. These developments, as we have seen, emphasise connectedness over autonomy, processes over products, and systems over details. Stability and routines are out: the next new thing is what matters, and not just to young people. Most importantly, these developments emphasise difference, diversity, and plurality over homogeneity and sameness. They represent a very deep and real challenge to our current ways of doing things in education. They are deeply unsettling to our one-size-fits-all, assembly-line style of schooling that, by offering every student the same pre-packaged knowledge, in the same order, at the same time, aims to turn them out as clones. Teachers and parents have good reasons to feel defensive. However, as I have argued throughout this book, if we do nothing and wait for all this to go away, we will not be preparing young people for life in the knowledge society. I think we should not see these developments as a threat to everything we value in education, but as an opportunity to reshape our mental model of education, and it is in this context that the ideas from post-modern theory we discussed earlier become useful. In the next section, I explore, by discussing some of the issues arising out of recent debates about the role of ICTs in schools, not only how we might use these ideas to reshape our mental model of education but also what we could do differently in our schools to better prepare students for the knowledge age.

EDUCATION FOR THE DIGITAL AGE?

Recent published work on the future of schooling has a lot to say about the role of ICTs in schools. For many authors, the knowledge age and ICTs are virtually synonymous. ICTs are seen as a magic bullet that will revolutionise teaching and learning. However, if we look more closely at how these authors think this will happen, we can see that these claims are not very convincing. The first thing to notice is that the ICTs they talk about are not the kind that involve text messaging, MSN, chat rooms, online gaming, or downloading music videos. Rather, the focus, in general, is on using ICTs to do more or less what schools have always done, but doing it better, faster, and in ways that are more appealing to students. The thinking is that, through ICTs, learners can be connected to vast amounts of information, and be part of a worldwide network of learners. Furthermore, ICTs in schools are an important way of bridging the "digital divide". Using ICT, these resources can be offered to a wide range of people who would not otherwise have access to them, and these people can acquire the computer-related skills that, we are told, are now essential in the employment market place.

Schools have responded to these discussions by developing "information literacy" programmes, teaching students about the Internet, and designing tasks that students can tackle using information available on websites (with the help of online resources provided by their teachers). This is digital "busy work". However, it is valued because students are using technologies that have a high status in the world outside school, and this, it seems, must be a good thing.

These approaches, when looked at in terms of how they are educating students for life in the knowledge age, have important flaws. First, and most obviously, the information learners have access to isn't knowledge in either the old sense of the term, or, as I argue in the next chapter, in the new sense. Second, having access to large amounts of information doesn't necessarily lead to large amounts of learning. Without a clear context for accessing this information, students quickly experience information overload. Third, while there is a lot of talk about learning, there is very little discussion of *what*—if anything—students need to learn and/or *why* they might need to learn it. As far as I can tell, it seems to be assumed that students will learn more or less the same kinds of things they have always learned *or* that it doesn't really matter what they are learning as long as they are learning *something*.

Worse, however, this approach misses the point entirely in terms of what is significant about the new age. All the talk about information—the information revolution and so on—deflects attention from what really matters in the new age, which isn't information at all. What is really significant is the relationships between people, and between people and organisations, that are made possible by the new modes of communication. It also takes attention away from knowledge, in particular the new meaning of knowledge that is the defining feature of the knowledge age. This new meaning is entirely missing from the current focus on ICTs in schools, and we are consequently losing the opportunity to develop the incredible educational potential of these technologies.

Current approaches will do little to revolutionise teaching and learning. Although they may encourage the development of individualised learning packages that will allow students to work at different levels at a pace that suits them when learning such basic skills as multiplication tables or spelling, these strategies, on their own, are hardly effective for building capacity to participate in the knowledge society. In addition, seeing ICTs as tools for gathering and processing information and/or becoming part of some giant learning network is highly unlikely to be an effective strategy for raising the educational achievement of currently disadvantaged groups. I think it is likely to have the opposite effect, for a number of reasons.

First, if we assume that students will learn more or less the same kinds of things they have always learned, then teachers will continue to develop learning programmes that are designed to focus students' information-gathering efforts around the old, objective, finished kinds of knowledge that are the basis of the traditional curriculum. However, as we all know, large numbers of students don't find this kind of knowledge engaging. They experience it as distant, remote, and impersonal, as having nothing much to do with them and their immediate concerns. This, of course, is not a new issue, but using computers to access this kind of knowledge will not, on its own, be a successful strategy for engaging these students in learning. If we think students need this kind of knowledge (and I think they do), then we need to develop new strategies for engaging them (Chapter 6 looks at some of the possibilities).

Second, today's school students are likely to have experienced multimedia and Internet-based ICTs in non-educational contexts. Many will be far more comfortable with these multi-modal technologies than they are with the print-based technologies that underlie traditional school knowledge. While they may be familiar with the technologies being used, it doesn't necessarily follow that their information-gathering activities will result in the kind of learning their teachers expect. Furthermore, *because* they are familiar with these technologies, they are likely to find this way of using them old-fashioned, boring, and alien. Quite apart from anything else, the software they are likely to be using in educational contexts is light years behind even the most basic gaming software in terms of the quality of its visuals and its ability to excite and engage.

Third, if we assume that it doesn't really matter what they are learning as long as they are learning something, then we are likely to encourage students to follow their own interests and develop their own individualised programmes of learning. Schools will quickly become just one among many information sources available to students and will have to compete with these other sources for the learners' attention.

Some students will learn a great deal more than others, and it will become harder and harder to justify having a public education system. If we want our education system to provide the resources we need for economic growth and build social cohesion, then we will have to do better than this. We need a framework that will give everyone enough understanding of the world and how it works to contribute to it and, where necessary, transform it.

Because education's purpose is to prepare people for the world they will live in, it must be future focused. The current approach to ICTs in education is not future focused, and nor is it especially innovative. Rather, it is an "old knowledge" strategy, designed to recapitulate the world of the past rather than lay the foundations for the world of the future. In the end, it will fail. What should we do instead then? How *can* we think about education in ways that take account of the new orientation to knowledge and identity? The good news is that we don't have to start at square one. Out there in specialised corners of educational research, are people working on these very questions right now. The not so good news is that their ideas aren't widely known among classroom teachers, and because they represent a major mind-shift in how we think about education, it will probably be a while before they are widely understood. However, it is through these ideas, and other ideas like them, that we will be able to build a genuinely future-focused education system. I want to end this chapter with a brief look at this work. I don't have space to do more than provide a flavour of these ideas, but there are plenty of references in the notes at the end of the chapter if you want to read more.

MULTI-MODAL LITERACIES AND DIGITAL EPISTEMOLOGIES

The body of work I outline here has its origins in literacy education, linguistics, and media studies, but, for reasons that will become clear shortly, it has expanded well beyond those fields. It charts the changes in knowledge and representation that are now a feature of the world outside education, argues that a major shift in thinking is needed inside education, and suggests how we might go about producing this shift. The new ICTs play an important role in all this.

This work argues that the replacement of the standard view of knowledge by the new digitised knowledges and multimedia forms of representation has major implications for what we do in schools. The standard view of knowledge arises out of, and is deeply embedded in, print culture. It is propositional knowledge, expressed in and organised by the conventions of written text. This "knowing that" kind of knowledge is the basis of school knowledge. In schools, "knowing how" has always been subordinate to knowing that, even in the so-called practical subjects. The exception is the all-important knowing how to read and write. It is because school knowledge and written text are so deeply interconnected that learning how to read and write has been so important. Written texts are organised in ways that reflect, and are reflected in, the organisation of propositional knowledge. This organisation, which originates in how we talk, has a sequential, time-based logic. One statement is made, followed by a second one, and so on. One thing is thus first, another is second, and another will have to be last.

Meaning is attached to being first and being last, and this meaning is understood by any competent user of this language/knowledge system. Understanding how and why meaning systems like this work has traditionally been an important goal of literacy education programmes.

Schools emphasise text-based meaning and the knowledges that are associated with it. These are, however, not the only ways of producing meaning, and in today's world, they are no longer the dominant ways. Meaning—and thus knowledge—is increasingly being produced in other ways, ways that school students need to know about if they are to be well prepared for life in this world. Language and text are no longer the main ways we represent and/or communicate ideas. Today, visual symbols—images, graphs, diagrams, symbols, gestures, 3D objects, and so on—are becoming more important than print, and the screen is taking over from the book as the main medium for representing and communicating ideas.

This change is highly significant for educationists in *all* subject areas. An image's meaning is produced differently from a text's meaning, because the rules for organising it are different. The parts of an image are not ordered in time as a sequence, but are organised in space, as a depiction or a display. The image's meaning is achieved via the placement of the parts. For example, placing something at the centre means that something else will be on the margins. Placing something at the top of the available space means that it will be above something else, and so on. This placement will have a meaning that will be communicated to anyone who is literate in the meaning system of which the image is a part.

Thus, reading a text is one kind of literacy; reading an image is another. Each mode of communication has different rules and requirements, and each mode organises, and constructs, the world differently. The world told, or narrated, is a very different world from the world shown, or depicted.

There are, of course, other modes of representation—sounds, music, movements, smells even—all of which are deployed in today's meaning systems. However, the really significant development is that *multi*-modal representation is now common. Words, images, and sounds are now routinely presented together. The words, images, and sounds communicate different things, but the combination of all three communicates things that each could not do on its own. To understand today's world, it is no longer enough to be formally literate in only one meaning system—the text-based, propositional knowledge system. We need to be able to read and write in many different modes, and to be able to read messages spread across many modes simultaneously.

If constructing meaning is now multi-modal, it makes sense to use ICTs to develop young people's literacy in these different modes. Literacy education programmes could then draw young people's knowledge of these technologies into their education, not set it apart from them. For example, James-Paul Gee, in his book *What Video Games Have to Teach us about Learning and Literacy*, makes a powerful case for seeing video games not as mindless entertainment but as intricate learning experiences requiring high levels of literacy in a number of important domains. Successful video games, he argues, incorporate many of the principles of successful learning (engagement, motivation, and scaffolding for example), principles that we could and should use in designing school learning activities. It also makes sense to go beyond using ICTs as a means of gathering information that is later used to reconstruct old knowledge. Instead, these resources should be used to build the kind of *relationships* that are necessary if schools are to be knowledge producers, rather than knowledge consumers as they are now.

NEW METAPHORS

To get underway with initiatives like this in our schools, we need to replace the industrial-age, assembly-line metaphor with a metaphor that works in the knowledge-age context—one that is based on the idea of a system, or a network, that has multiple possibilities, multiple connections, and multiple pathways. Others have attempted to do just this in other contexts. For example, it is now common to see social, political, economic, and commercial phenomena represented not as machines, as they might have been in the past, but as organisms or living systems. In line with this analogy, the phenomenon being studied is seen as a complex set of interconnected and interdependent parts, as a whole that is greater than the sum of its parts. Thus understanding the relationships between the system's various parts, not the parts themselves, is the key to understanding the system.

A biological metaphor I have found helpful is the concept of a clade. Biologists use the term clade, derived from a Greek word meaning the branch of a tree, to refer to the unspecialised groups of organisms that colonise the new environments created when a catastrophic event upsets the balance of nature. The offspring of these generalised organisms diversify and specialise to form a whole variety of new and different species. A clade is thus an organism that has the capacity to develop in any number of different ways. Evolutionarily speaking, a clade is the opposite of a clone. A clone is an exact copy of its parent organism. It can only function successfully in the environment for which it is specialised; it has no means of adapting to the new environment. Clades are the foundation of great leaps forward in evolution, while clones are evolutionary dead ends. For biologists, clades represent diversity, dynamism, innovation, and ongoing life, while clones signify conformity, constriction, and eventual death. Our schools, as industrial-age institutions, are set up to produce clones—conformist, rule-following copies, who faithfully reproduce what is given to them. However, we are now at a point in history where the "balance of nature" of our past is being seriously disrupted. If the products of our schools are to flourish in the new environment, they need the capacity to develop along any one of a number of different branches, and the capacity to decide for themselves which branches to follow.

ADJUSTING OUR MENTAL MODELS

At the beginning of this chapter, I outlined a simple mental model of education that underlies our thinking about what education is, and what it is for. The principles on which this model is based are, in most cases, still sound and worth defending, but some of its features need adjusting if it is to work for us in the post-modern era. The parts that need adjusting are those that have to do with education's role in producing equal opportunity and social cohesion.

In the past, people thought that social cohesion was best built by giving everyone, from all classes and cultures and both sexes, the opportunity to aspire to the same goals. Everyone could, if they worked hard, own a house, have a family, own a car, and/or any number of other standardised consumer products. Our national system of compulsory education would give everyone the skills needed to get a job and participate in this dream. Through this standardising of desire, we would achieve a conflict-free society where everyone had a place and was happy in that place. In this dream, we would all be the same, and this would be a good thing. But as is well known, this dream has never been realised, mainly because it requires all groups to be assimilated under one mantle, a mantle that we assumed (although never talked about explicitly) to be the norm. Post-modern political theorists have come up with an alternative model of social cohesion based on difference, not sameness. Rather than repressing difference and trying to make it invisible, this model celebrates it. It brings it out into the open, and gives it a place to stand, not so that it can be assimilated but so that it can express itself, on its own terms.

What would this model look like if we tried to use it as the basis for our education system? Would it work? If we seriously attempted to implement it, wouldn't we just end up in a situation where anything goes, where anyone could say they wanted to be anything, or do anything, and this would be fine? Would this matter? Well, yes, it would matter, mainly because it would disadvantage the very people who most need the education system's support. However, I think it is possible to take up the "difference" model without necessarily producing a situation in which anything goes. To do this, I think it is important that we do not start talking about diversity *instead* of equality in an *ad hoc* way until we have thought carefully about what this means. Instead, I think that we need, to return to our old mental model of education and to rework it to fit better with the new conception of individuality.

The liberal ideal of education is an important cornerstone of the old mental model. According to this ideal, education's purpose is to develop people's natural capacity for reason by exposing them to the best and greatest knowledge our civilisation has produced. Studying this knowledge—the knowledge that is the basis of the subjects of the traditional academic curriculum—helps people to understand how society and the natural world work. It helps them to learn from the lessons of history and to appreciate the finer things in life. Studying these subjects is difficult. Young learners do not always appreciate what they don't know, and so a certain amount of order and discipline is necessary if they are to learn these things. Schools thus require young learners to submit to the discipline of the subject and the discipline of their teacher.

If students do this, they will become the kinds of people that these subjects are supposed to make them—rational, disciplined, and respectful of authority. At the same time, however, they will also develop their own authority. Studying these subjects will bring out their natural reason, to the point where, intellectually (as opposed to physically) speaking, they are adults, people able to think for themselves independently of the authority of others, able to make choices about how they want to live their lives, and, importantly, able to defend and justify those choices to others. This is the goal of the traditional liberal education. It is a model that is quite unashamedly knowledge centred, and it is a model that requires people to submit to the authority of this knowledge before they can develop their own authority. Some people find it easier than others to submit, possibly because what they are submitting to meshes well with other aspects of their lives, or possibly because they want what is promised to them if they go through with this process. Whatever the reason, the choice is clear: agree to submit and be assimilated into all that goes with that knowledge, or drop out.

This model, as it stands, is clearly not an appropriate basis for a post-modern education system—because it is incapable of taking account of diversity. As I have tried to show in this chapter, difference and diversity are key features of post-modern thought. There are many different ways of being, and these ways of being are made possible in the discourses we inhabit. A person's identity is no longer seen as a stable, coherent whole but as a complex multiplicity of subjectivities that are immersed and constructed in discourses, and in the subjectivities of others. If people are to function successfully in this new age, they need the capacity to be many things (to be clades, not clones). They also need to know how to manage these different ways of being. They need to be able to operate successfully in a range of different discourses and to move easily between them. They need to understand the rules of different discourses well enough to be able to use them, modify them, and, where necessary, invent new ones. They need to understand how their sense of self is produced in discourse, to appreciate that it is different in different discourses, and to realise that if they understand the rules of the game sufficiently well, they can play with this sense of self and modify it. In other words, they need to be discourse literate: to be able to *read* discourses at many levels—on, between, and beyond the lines.

People have always needed to know these things, and educators have always tried to teach them (although they have given them different names). In the past, however, teachers tried to develop this fluency with discourses by exposing students to certain kinds of knowledge. Self-understanding and understanding of the wider social system, it was thought, would follow. But this hasn't necessarily followed, and in the new age, self-understanding and systems-level understanding probably now need to come first. How we do this in a principled way that doesn't require people to submit to the disciplines and be assimilated is a concern. One possible way takes us back to the liberal ideal of education. Its end goal—developing intellectual adulthood—is a goal that I think is worth preserving, although, in the new era, we need a new way of getting there. In the past, this goal was probably more of an ideal than a reality. From Plato's time onwards, intellectual adulthood has been something only really achieved by an élite. Most people do not in fact break free of the authority of others and become fully self-determining as a result of their education. On the contrary, most learn to submit to authority, to follow rules, and to slot quietly into society somewhere. However, there are now economic and philosophical reasons why we *all* need to be able to think for ourselves, make choices for ourselves, and be able to explain to others why we made those choices. The development of intellectual adulthood can no longer depend on submission to the existing disciplines, but instead can be developed through the discourse literacy-based approach outlined above. This approach does not mean casting aside the old disciplines. They will still have a role of in the new order, as I explain in the next chapter.

NOTES

the current context

Page ***100***: Brodribb (1992) and Dawkins (1998) are two examples of work arguing that post-modernism means that "anything goes" or that "nothing matters".

Pages ***100–101***: Many of the words in this section ("investing" in a "quality" system in order to "grow" our pool of the "exceptionally talented", "raising everyone's game", and so on) are taken from recent government policy documents, especially the documents *Growing an Innovative New Zealand* (Prime Minister's Department, 2002) and Briefing to the Incoming Minister of Education (Ministry of Education, 2002a).

equality and education

Page ***101***: See "Further or Better? The legacy of 1877" in Openshaw, Lee, and Lee (1993), as well as Harker (1990), or Shuker (1987) for the debates that took place at the time of the passing of the 1877 Education Act.

The principle of equal educational opportunity was made explicit in the often quoted (and recently reaffirmed) "Beeby vision" for education in 20th century New Zealand. This term was recently used in publicity material for the Quality Education Coalition's 2003 conference Re-claiming Public Education. It refers to the statement, written by Dr C. E. Beeby, but made in Parliament in 1939 by the Prime Minister and Minister of Education Peter Fraser, outlining the First Labour Government's vision for education. This term was also used recently in the Prime Minister's speech to the 2003 Knowledge Wave conference; in her speech at the launch of the Tertiary Education Commission in February 2003; and in the Associate Minister of Education's speech The Beeby Vision Today, given at the Re-claiming Public Education conference in July 2003. (These speeches were, at the time of writing, available on the government's website: www.beehive.govt.nz). However, as Beeby himself acknowledged, this vision was basically "a useful myth" (see Beeby, 1986).

our mental models of education

Pages ***102–103***: School improvement theorists (see, for example, Barber, 1996; Slavin, 1996; Slavin et al., 1994) argue that all schools could make a major difference to people's life chances by improving the quality of what they offer. Other educationists argue that it is unfair and unrealistic to expect schools to overcome the effects of disadvantage without major support from other agencies. See, for example, Mortimore and Whitty, (1997), Thrupp, (1999, 2000), Thrupp, Mansell, Hawksworth and Harold, (2003). See also Anyon (1997) and Thomson (2002), two recent books on schooling in disadvantaged areas that do not blame the schools or the students. Academic work that takes a strong view on the first position—that there will always be people who will not achieve well in school because of individual deficiencies (in ability or work habits, for example)—is less common (but see Herrnstein and Murray, 1994), and highly controversial. However, it is implicit in a great deal of educational thinking.

Page ***104***: The idea that we should ask a different question comes from the work of the British educational psychologist Valerie Walkerdine (on the problem of girls and mathematics). Her work, in turn, uses ideas from the work of the French philosopher Michel Foucault. See, especially, her book *Counting Girls Out* (Walkerdine, 1989) and the collaboration *Changing the Subject* (Henriques, Hollway, Urwin, Venn, and Walkerdine, 1984).

where does our mental model of education come from?

Pages **104–105**: Accounts of the modern conception of individuality can be found in any introductory politics text, but the references I used were Anchor (1967), Cassirer (1955), MacPherson (1962), and Seidman (1983).

so what's missing?

Pages **105–107**: For an analysis of the modern individual as head of household and the consequential exclusion of women and other dependants from individuality, see Pateman (1988, 1989) and Yeatman (1994, 2000). For more general feminist critiques of modern political thought, see Eisenstein (1981), Elshtain (1981), Flax (1990, 1992) and Gutmann (1980). As Anna Yeatman observes, "some [individuals] are more 'individual' than others, most being under the private control of others who are more effectively individualised than themselves" (Yeatman, 1994, p. 78).

Pages **107-108**: Valerie Walkerdine (1988, 1989) shows clearly how, in educational contexts, *difference* means *deficient*. Diana Sartori (1994) shows how woman—in political, economic, and intellectual contexts—is represented as being "not the real thing", a "poor substitute" for man. Genevieve Lloyd's 1993 book *The Man of Reason* demonstrates that the individual knower, or subject, of knowledge has, since the time of the Ancient Greek philosophers, always been a *masculine* subject, and Evelyn Fox Keller's (1985) book *Reflections on Gender and Science* shows how inextricably connected science and masculinity are.

Pages **107–108**: For critiques of identity politics and the essentialism it implies, see Fuss (1989) or Riley (1988). Walzer (1983), Yeatman (1993), Yeatman and Gunew (1993), and Young (1990a 1990b) all make the case for what they call the "politics of difference". Some authors refer to this rethinking of politics as the "third way" because it doesn't fit easily with traditional political understandings of left and right. This term is, however, controversial. Giddens (1998) argues that the third way does not lie beyond left and right, but that it is part of the left, and part of a move to resuscitate and renew old ideas about social democracy. This is how I see it—hence the title of this chapter. For discussions of how, within modern political thought, it is logically impossible to claim equality *and* difference, see Rancière (1992) or Yeatman (1994). Scott (2003) argues that the equality-versus-difference antithesis hides the interdependence of the two terms, and, that deconstructing it moves the debate beyond the constraints of the standard terms of modern political thought.

being equal *and* different

Pages ***109–111***: Diana Fuss, in *Essentially Speaking*, argues that deconstructing a concept is, on its own, sufficient to produce a change in how that concept works. Yeatman (1994), Yeatman and Wilson (1995), and Young (1990, 1992) all discuss the concept of "working difference together". The notion of the "saturated self" comes from Gergen (1991). See also Giddens (1991).

many ways of being: subjectivity and discourse

Pages ***111–113***: The approach to discourse outlined in this chapter has its origins in the work of the French philosopher Michel Foucault, particularly his 1972 book *The Archaeology of Knowledge*.

Page ***112***: The discourse of developmental psychology is specifically discussed in this way in Walkerdine (1984, 1988). See also the later work of other critical psychologists, for example, Burman (1994), Harre and Gillett (1994), Henriques et al. (1984), Morss (1996), and Parker (1992). This work aims to redefine the traditional objects of psychology—human subjectivity, social behaviour, mind and intelligence—not as biological properties of individual bodies, but as discursive constructs. While not all critical psychologists see themselves as post-modernists, their work is nevertheless part of what is known as the post-modern "turn".

Page **114**: The notion of hybridity first developed in post-modern theory to identify and understand the patterns of ethnic identity that seemed to be emerging in the new post-colonial, globalised world. See, for example, Bhabha, (1984, 1990, 1996), Blair and Holland, (1995), Brah, (1996), Donald and Rattansi, (1992), Gilroy, (1993), Hall, (1992), Trinh Minh-ha, (1988), Tsolidis (2001). "Border crossing", "border existences", the "*mestiza*" (Anzualdúa, 1987), "liminality" (Grossberg, 1996) and the "third space" (Bhabha 1990) are allied concepts, developed to map hybrid existence. The slash/suture motif is often used to express the idea of "working difference together", that is, acknowledging difference *as difference* (not lack or deficiency), while also acknowledging commonalities and points of agreement. See, for example, Jagose (1993), Yeatman (1993). The idea of subjectivity as a verb, not a noun, comes from Flax (1996, see p. 578). For accounts of the blurring of the distinction between being an actor and being acted on, see Flax (1990, 1993), Lugones (1982, 1994) and Scheman (1996). The quote about the *mestiza* identity accepting all of its parts is taken from Anzualdúa (1987, pp. 79, 88).

identity in the real world

Pages **116–118**: According to Jameson (1991), post-modern society is consumer driven. He says that people's identity is now determined not through social class but their market location and the particular niche products they choose. We are, he says, nothing more than "desiring machines". Catherine Lumby, in her book *Gotcha* (1999), argues that the merging of the old "highbrow" media and the tabloids into "infotainment" has remodelled the traditional public sphere, and is producing new, more democratic, forms of public life. For discussions of people's use of virtual communities to "play" with identity, see Gee (2003) or Turkle (1997).

Pages **118–119**: Kenway and Bullen (2001) discuss the "moral panic" response of many teachers and parents to children's immersion in cyber-culture.

education for the digital age?

Pages ***119–120***: For recent policy discussions of ICTs and education, see the Ministry of Education's (1998) *Interactive Education* and 2002b *Information and Communication Technologies Strategy for Schools*, or the Information Technology Advisory Group's (1999) report to the Minister of Education. Perelman (1992) makes the case that ICTs will eventually replace schools, while Cuban (2001) and Oppenheimer (2003) are two recent books that argue strongly against the uncritical use of computers in schools. Bigum (2003) makes an interesting case for using ICTs to allow schools to be knowledge-producing rather than knowledge-consuming entities. See also Oblinger and Oblinger (2005).

multi-modal literacies and digital epistemologies

Pages ***124–127***: The new literacy studies and/or multi-literacies literature is huge. The ideas outlined on these pages came from Gee (2003), Kress (2003), and Lankshear and Knobel (2003). However, see also Cope and Kalantsis (2000), Gee (1992, 1996), Lankshear (1999), and Lankshear, Peters and Knobel (2000). The concept of digital epistemologies comes from Lankshear and Knobel (2000). The idea that we live in an information-rich age in which attention is now the scarce resource is from Lankshear and Knobel (2002).

new metaphors

Pages ***127–128***: For work that treats knowledge, and the world in general, as if it were a complex biological system, see Capra (1983, 1996), Davies (1983, 1989), Dyson (1981), Margulis and Sagan (1995), Maturana and Varela (1997), and Varela, Thompson and Rosch (1991). The clade metaphor is taken from Dyson (1981) and used by Hedley Beare and Richard Slaughter to argue that our schools need to "develop multiple forms and living branches" if they are not to move closer towards death (Beare, 2001). But see also Beare and Slaughter, (1993), Slaughter (1989).

adjusting our mental models

Page **132**: The three-level notion of reading (on, between, and beyond the lines) comes from Herber, cited in Morris and Stewart-Dore (1984, p. 98). Devine (2003) is an interesting article that explores the idea of teaching as a process of actively creating identities or subjectivities.

CHAPTER 6

DOES KNOWLEDGE MATTER?

RECENTLY, PEOPLE HAVE STARTED TO WRITE ABOUT WHAT the knowledge society means for schools. This work, which is mainly addressed to policy makers and educational leaders, talks mostly about the physical and organisational changes that are needed. It says that the schools of the future will be managed differently from those of today. Student learning will be organised differently and teachers' work will be very different. The single-site, self-contained schools of today will be replaced by multi-campus entities that are designed to work closely with other agencies and community organisations, and the standard industrial-age classroom will be replaced by more flexible learning spaces that allow students and teachers to work together in a range of different ways.

SO, WHAT, SPECIFICALLY, ARE THESE PEOPLE SAYING?

They foresee the current focus on delivering a sequential, one-size-fits-all curriculum to batches of students giving way to individualised learning plans that allow individual students to work at a level and pace appropriate for them, and to achieve their goals via a variety of pathways. The curriculum will be an integrated network of possibilities, delivered in modular form on an as-and-when-needed basis—often off site. Schools will be open for business for longer hours, but students and teachers won't have to be present for all of that time. Schools and teachers will no longer be the sole providers of education for most students: instead, they will function as "learning brokers" for their students. Their aim will be to connect students of all ages with whomever, or whatever, best meets their particular learning needs.

These people also think that the learning programmes of the future will emphasise thinking, learning, and problem-solving skills. The aim will be to develop creativity, ingenuity, the ability to innovate, and the ability to work productively in groups. All this will take place in an ICT-rich environment, where the use of ICTs for information processing and research is routine.

Furthermore, these post-industrial-age schools will need teachers who have expertise in a diverse range of areas. Teachers will no longer be knowledge providers or supervisors, but learning managers. Their main job will be to ensure that every one of their students has a learning environment that works for them. They will design appropriate learning experiences for all their students, and guide them to appropriate sources of knowledge. To do this, teachers will need a well-developed knowledge of their teaching subject and how that subject is best taught. They will also need to know how to be a research supervisor, a group-work facilitator, and a problem poser. As individuals, they will need to be innovative, systems-level thinkers, who work well in cross-disciplinary teams. They will need to be strongly committed to their own ongoing learning, and to being part of several different professional learning communities, only some of which will include other teachers. They will need to be regular users of research knowledge in a wide range of areas—from work in their specialist subject area(s) and curriculum developments in that area, to work on how best to work with learners with widely varying backgrounds and needs.

One-size-fits-all approaches to teaching will no longer work. Teachers will need to be experts in packaging and repackaging what they know for increasingly diverse groups of learners in an increasingly diverse range of situations. They will probably work not in one school as most do now, but on a contract basis, on a number of different, but concurrent, projects. These projects will be at different stages of completion and spread over several different sites. Instead of a teacher's work identity being associated, as it is now, with the school they work at, or the subject(s) they teach, it will align with the particular portfolios of knowledge, gained from study or work experience, they will use to secure their next assignment. They will be paid a market rate for this work (which will, the writers in this area suggest, be considerably more than the rates teachers are currently paid as salaried employees).

Following post-industrial-age management practices, the schools of the future will be managed as learning organisations, which means they will strive to continuously improve the quality of the services they offer to those who consume them (learners, in other words). Everyone involved in a school—its teachers, its students, the principal and other school leaders, its board of trustees, its administrative, technical, and support staff—will be regularly involved in programmes designed to upskill, retrain, or expand their existing knowledge base into new areas. Everyone will be involved in developing the big picture of where the school as a whole is going, and where each of them, as a part of that whole, is going. There will also be a strong focus on developing everyone's capacity for lifelong learning, particularly so for the students, but also for all others involved with the school.

Lifelong learning is not a new idea, but it is strongly emphasised in the knowledge-society literature. It is used as an umbrella term for anything that makes it possible for people to learn whatever they need to learn whenever they need to learn it, that is, at any age, and not necessarily in a formal education system. The literature stresses that the capacity for lifelong learning is necessary not only for participation in the new global economies but also for improving social cohesion, by ensuring fairer income distribution and reducing crime. It also says that, if we are to develop everyone's ability to be a lifelong learner, we need to adopt new approaches to teaching and learning. Formal education's traditional focus on abstract brain work needs to be supplanted with approaches that are more learner centred and contextual—"hands-on" approaches that involve real-world investigations and problem solving, innovation, and teamwork. We also need to provide people with more flexible learning opportunities, by increasing the availability of part-time, distance and e-learning programmes, for example, and making it easier for people to mix and match courses from different providers, both public and private, and at multiple levels.

The influence of the business management literature is clear here. There is a strong focus on "learning skills". *How* people learn, we are told, is now more important than *what* they learn. This shift, away from what we once called knowledge to an emphasis on skills or competencies is an interesting development. It is interesting, given that the knowledge society's defining feature is supposed to be its focus on knowledge, and on new and different ways of thinking about it. At first glance, the focus on skills might seem logical, given knowledge's new meaning as something active, or something that does things. However, emphasising learning skills over knowledge implies that knowledge doesn't matter any more. If this is the case, it is a significant development. However, it could be that the whole question of knowledge—what it actually is, whether or not it matters, and whether or not there is anything that everyone should learn—is being put into the "too-hard" basket. While it is not difficult to see why this might happen (the issues raised are, after all, difficult and have plagued educational thinking for a very long time), these questions are *the* issues that must be addressed if we are to have an education system that is capable of preparing people for life in the knowledge-based societies of the future.

The emphasis on learning skills sidesteps these issues. It is based on a partial understanding of the new meaning of knowledge, and it is an approach that, while it might work adequately in business contexts, is far from adequate as a framework for the schools of the future. Learning how to learn and learning about one's own learning are obviously important skills, in schools and in the workplace. Moreover, it is clearly important for us to rethink many of our ideas about how best to manage schools, and to rethink many of our practices in the light of the opportunities that are now available through new developments in ICT. However, the current literature's emphasis on these things puts the cart before the horse. Given the importance of the relationship between knowledge and education in past education systems, and given most people's understanding of knowledge, this emphasis can only lead to confusion.

The remainder of this chapter looks at some of the reasons why the focus on learning skills is not a good basis for preparing people for 21st century life. It explores the implications of knowledge's new meaning for the old meaning (the one our schools were built on), its implications for curriculum development and its implications for teaching and learning. As will become clear, I think that the old knowledges *will* matter in the education systems of the future, and it will matter *what* people learn. However, for reasons that I outline later in this chapter, I think that *why* these things will matter in the future will be very different from why they mattered in the past. But before we get onto this, I think it is useful to first look at why people might want to put these questions aside, in the too-hard basket.

WHY THE KNOWLEDGE QUESTION IS BEING AVOIDED

Education and knowledge are, for obvious reasons, intimately bound up with each other. Their histories are intertwined, and while there have been significant changes in the meanings of both over time, they remain closely connected. However, educational thinking about knowledge is rather muddled. It is a mixture of ideas, assumptions, and rituals, some of which we have inherited from past ages, and some that we have imported from other disciplines. Educationists do not have a single, coherent theory of knowledge. We don't have an agreed-on way to decide what we think knowledge *is*—how we think it develops, what good knowledge is, and so on. Instead, we have a hotchpotch of assumptions and ideas that, because they come from different philosophical traditions, often conflict. We use the term knowledge all the time in educational discussions, and it is clearly central to all educational activity. Most people think they know what it means, but, as is the case with many things, one person's meaning is not necessarily the same as another's. One thing is clear: there are many different ideas about what we should teach in schools, and why it is important. Given this muddle, it is hardly surprising that we have been reluctant to deal with the challenges posed by knowledge's new meaning, preferring instead to focus on more concrete issues, such as the new physical structures and people-management strategies that 21st century schools will need.

This issue of what knowledge means in education is not new, of course. However, it has been thrown into sharp relief by the advent of the knowledge society. We have needed a coherent theory of knowledge for a long time, but now the need is even more pressing. We need a theory that can help us decide whether knowledge matters in the schools of the future, and, if it does, what forms of knowledge matter and how best to develop them. This theory needs to take account of recent developments in knowledge, particularly, but not solely, the developments known as the knowledge society. It needs to fit with the goals of education, in general, and public education, in particular. It also needs to be capable of allowing difference. It must allow us to know in different ways, while at the same time allowing us to decide if a piece of knowledge *is* knowledge, whether it has value as knowledge (by being, for example, true, objective, robust, or useful). In short, we need a theory of knowledge that not only takes into account the changes signalled in the knowledge society literature but also offers something richer and more widely applicable than the business-oriented model presented there. If this sounds like a tall order, it probably is.

This chapter explores some of the features this new theory needs. It does not aim to provide a complete map of this new theory: that would need a whole new book. Rather, its goal is to raise issues and suggest some possible directions. However, before we look at what this new theory of knowledge might be like, I want to return to the question of why a focus on learning skills will not be a good basis for a knowledge society education system. I do this not because I have anything against the idea of learning skills but because the debate that this issue provokes provides a useful framework for exploring what is at stake—and what is missing—in recent discussions of what the knowledge society means for schools.

WHY LEARNING SKILLS ARE NOT ENOUGH

As discussed earlier, in the business world, knowledge, and innovation are closely linked ideas. Innovation is the process of producing new knowledge by using, and replacing, old knowledge. This new knowledge is not a thing, but something that *does* things, something that acts on things to produce new things. The policy literature's emphasis on learning skills is superficially consistent with this new meaning of knowledge, in that what people learn is apparently not important. Rather, the focus is on learning *per se*—learning as doing, learning as change, and learning as a generalised set of skills. However, for many reasons, this is a very weak strategy for dealing with the challenges posed by knowledge-society developments. Learner-centred, contextual, and/or hands-on approaches are not new in education, and skills-based approaches have been in widespread use, particularly in vocational forms of education, for a very long time. While these ideas have been less common in academic forms of education, there are good reasons for this, some of which I will explore shortly. All these ideas have histories: they bring with them baggage that, if not acknowledged, will be quite unhelpful in the new environment. Seizing on these approaches as the answer to the educational issues raised by knowledge's new meaning is an *ad hoc* response. It avoids dealing with the deeper issues raised by this new meaning, and so is unlikely to be successful. Something much more is needed.

There are many reasons why a curriculum that emphasises learning skills over knowledge is not a good strategy for bringing about the kind of changes we are looking for. I want to look at two of these reasons here. At first glance, these reasons look quite different. However, they are related. The first reason is that various lobby groups in education—important and powerful ones—will oppose this strategy for reasons that, when looked at in their historical context, are very good ones. Because of this opposition, the strategy will be only partially implemented, its success will be limited, and the assumptions and values driving the opposition will be left unchallenged. The second reason is that the strategy does not deal with the deeper issues raised by the change in knowledge's meaning, issues that are highly significant for the future of education. These two reasons are explored in more detail below.

WHY THE FOCUS ON LEARNING SKILLS WILL BE OPPOSED

Debate about almost any educational issue is invariably vigorous and usually politicised. This is especially the case when the issue involves changing some aspect of our national education system, which, because it is publicly funded, is supposed to meet the needs of everyone. Many different interest groups participate in these debates, often bringing ideas that come from radically different value systems. Everyone is an expert, because everyone, at some stage in their lives, has been to school. Argument is vociferous, entrenched positions develop, and there is generally a certain amount of mud slinging and name calling on all sides. Eventually, a compromise of some sort is reached. This usually satisfies no one and, once implemented, it produces outcomes that are, at best, confused. In general, people just go back to doing more or less what they have always done.

At one level, this happens because the debate is political. Any educational debate has important implications for the allocation of resources and so is usually a power struggle. At another level, however, this pattern of debate happens because our education system is underpinned by many different ideas, each with different origins and so often in conflict with one another. These ideas have, nevertheless, existed alongside each other for a very long time. As we saw in Chapter 3, the way our education system developed, means that some important tensions are built into it. For example, there is a tension between the need to prepare people for economic participation and the need to prepare them for participation in civil society. There are tensions between meeting individual needs and meeting the needs of society, and there are tensions between academic and applied knowledge, and between rigour and inclusiveness.

For more than a century, these tensions have framed curriculum debates. New initiatives always try to achieve a balance, which satisfies no one. They are always a mixture of ideas, many of which contradict each other. For example, whenever a new, more inclusive or more learner-centred curriculum is proposed, the advocates of traditional academic forms of education complain that it lacks rigour and/or that it encourages people to think that anything goes. The proponents of inclusiveness, on the other hand, claim that the traditional curriculum is elitist and conservative. They say that it only meets the needs of a tiny minority of the population, and that it plays a major role in reproducing existing social inequalities. Whenever administrators try to introduce a curriculum that emphasises knowledge, skills, and values that are deemed to be useful and relevant in the real world outside education, advocates of traditional liberal education—whether conservative or progressive—oppose it. They argue that a public education system's main goal is to build social cohesion by laying the foundations for people's participation in civil society, not to provide the economy with its human resource needs. The administrators, on the other hand, are likely to argue that a crucial precursor for participation in civil society is the ability to participate in the economy, that is, to have a job. Because this is the first and most basic need, they say, the core goal of a public education system is to ensure that everyone has sufficient basic literacy and numeracy skills to get a job. Some would argue that, once this basic need has been met, any further education is a private individual benefit, not a core state responsibility.

This debate reflects a long-standing pattern. Because of this, we should expect a similar response to the idea of using skills-based and/or learner-centred approaches in all forms of education. This idea will be strongly contested by many educationists (and by others in the wider public sphere). Skills-based, contextually-focused, hands-on, learner-centred approaches to education have, in the past, been strongly associated with non-academic forms of education. They are widely thought of as being diametrically opposed to the more didactic, discipline-oriented approaches usually associated with the academic curriculum, as being more appropriate for use with low-ability students, and as lower in status. Because these approaches are widely used in vocational training, that is, to train people in certain highly specific and pre-determined skills, they are not regarded as appropriate for use in contexts where the goal is to develop the ability to think for oneself—in the sense meant by Plato. Traditionalists will oppose the use of these approaches because (they will say) standards and rigour will be sacrificed. Left-leaning educationists will oppose it because they will see it as evidence of the influence of New Right political philosophies—as education's capitulation to the demands of business. In other words, we will see a rehearsing of the same old arguments we always hear every time change is suggested.

These ideas, and the baggage that goes with them, are part of education's history and are deeply entrenched in educational thinking. Most people take them as given and rarely think about them at a conscious level. While these positions have flaws, each is more or less internally consistent and, in the context of an industrial-age education system, defensible. However in the new environment, this is no longer the case. We no longer have any *necessary* reason for teaching academic knowledge in the traditional way, but have many good reasons why it should *not* be taught this way. The old reasons no longer apply. However because this is not yet well understood, the current focus on learning skills will be resisted by those committed to traditional academic forms of knowledge. The divisions between academic and applied knowledge, rigour and inclusiveness, the economy and society are a feature of industrial-age approaches to education. If we are to develop post-industrial-age education we need to move beyond those divisions. We need to put academic and applied knowedge back together, to find ways to have rigour *and* inclusiveness, and to meet the needs of the economy and civil society. Why do we need to do this? We need to do this because what people need to be able to do with knowledge (and who needs to be able to do it) is now very different.

HOW WE WILL USE THE NEW MEANINGS OF KNOWLEDGE

Firstly, in the new environment, rather than being "stuff" that is made (usually by following certain rules) and stored away for future use, knowledge now "does stuff". Secondly, it produces new stuff. Rather than being something built on over time, it is something that produces change. Third, it develops through connections and relationships. It happens when people work collaboratively to solve specific problems—when they put their individual understandings of different knowledge systems together to generate new knowledge. Fourth, this new knowledge is contextual. It is considered good knowledge if it produces a workable solution to the problem, with the criteria used to judge the quality of the solution depending on the context in which the problem is being solved. These criteria differ from context to context. Marketing or industrial contexts have different criteria from situations involving "blue-sky" scientific research, for example. Knowledge's quality or value, is judged not according to whether it is true or objective, but whether it works in the particular local context. This context is important. Assessing knowledge's quality means taking account of the people who were involved, the brief they were given, the time and other resources they had available, and the strengths and limitations of that knowledge *vis-à-vis* its context. Fifth, knowledge is no longer divided into different disciplines and specialty areas. It is eclectic in that developing new knowledge involves taking elements from different disciplinary areas, putting them together with elements from other disciplinary areas, and rearranging them so that they have new meanings. This approach allows knowledge to *work* in different ways and *do* new things. This last feature is, I think, highly significant for educationists. It signals a way of thinking about knowledge that is obviously very different from the model on which our education system is built, and it gives us a framework for developing an educationally appropriate response to knowledge's changing meaning.

PLAYING WITH KNOWLEDGE: THE END OF DISCIPLINE(S)?

If we accept that knowledge's meaning is changing in the ways outlined above, and if we accept that one of the functions of schooling is to prepare people to live and work with this meaning, then our students need to acquire knowledge, but they also need to be able to *do* things with it. As the French philosopher Jean-François Lyotard puts it, they need the skills to "pursue performativity". By this, he means understanding old knowledge, not to reproduce it or follow its rules, but to use it to develop completely new knowledge. Thus, the new knowledge workers need to understand how different fields of old knowledge work—what is studied, how it is studied, what the different parts of the field are, how the parts fit together, and so on—but they also need to be systems-level thinkers. They need to be adept at putting elements taken from one knowledge system together with elements from another, arranging them so that they work in new ways and do new things. They need the ability to move easily between different knowledge systems, translating, and mediating between them as they go.

A school curriculum designed to prepare people for life in the knowledge society needs to help students see knowledge as a series of *connected systems* rather than a series of separate fields. Instead of understanding the detailed facts of, for example, science or history, students need to understand how science or history work as *systems*. The facts of science or history will still matter, as will knowing how scientists or historians work. Knowing about these things will be important not as an end goal, but because it develops understanding of science or history as systems. They will be examples of the kinds of knowledge produced when one works in that way.

Given this emphasis on performativity and systems-level understanding, it is clear that a knowledge-age education system needs to do much more than develop people's skills in learning, thinking, investigating, and solving problems. Learning, thinking, investigating, and so on do not happen in a vacuum. They require a context. Similarly, learners, thinkers, and investigators need raw materials—things to think about, learn, and investigate, things to do things with. They also need tools and strategies for thinking and learning, and these, too, will be different in different contexts. A learner's choice of tools and strategies will depend on what they are learning, thinking about, or investigating, and what they want to achieve as a result. Moreover, if they are to be lifelong learners, if they are to continue to develop and build on their existing repertoire of strategies for thinking, learning, investigating and problem solving, they need to know that *every* discipline offers them these strategies, and that they need experience in using the different thinking systems.

These ideas, so far, are not new. What is new is that, within the new environment, *all* students, not just those destined for academic careers, need to be able to think beyond the existing subjects, and, because the reasons for offering students this knowledge are now different, it needs to be packaged differently.

Traditional secondary school teachers are subject specialists who deliver their subject to students as a discrete package of facts and procedures, usually organised into topics or units of work. These facts and procedures are conventionally treated as finished bits of knowledge, knowledge that is authoritative, given and beyond question, and must be deferred to. (Learning a particular discipline involves being disciplined by it: one learns to think in ways that fit with that discipline.) The knowledge is valuable because it has stood the test of time; it is how things are. It is also valuable because it is the kind of knowledge an educated person knows. Students are encouraged to acquire it because it is good knowledge, because it will help them to better understand or appreciate the world around them, *or* because it will be useful to them (in some general non-specific way).

This approach constructs students as passive spectators, neophytes who, because they do not yet know enough to be allowed to actively participate in the knowledge system, are forced to wait on the sidelines, consuming and storing the already finished knowledge they are presented with. The vast majority never make it to the point (usually at post-graduate level) where they are allowed to participate in the process of building new knowledge. The result of this is that, for most people, knowledge is something they passively consume. They take no part in producing it; they are distant from it, uncommitted to it, and intimidated by it.

Educators have long lamented this situation, but it is a logical consequence of the industrial age ways of educating people, wherein specialist experts develop new knowledge and non-expert people only need to know enough to follow the rules and procedures involved in implementing it. Non-expert are not encouraged to understand the knowledge system and, although they might object to parts of it, they rarely try to change it. Rather, they try to find a place, within it or outside it, that they can fit into. Knowledge-based societies, however, need everyone, rather than a small élite, to be able to interact actively with knowledge. They require everyone to understand how different knowledge systems work, to be able to critique, manipulate, and transform existing knowledge, and to be able to explain what they have done to other people.

The challenge we face, of course, is getting our education system from where it is now to where it needs to be if it is to meet the needs of the knowledge age. We can't, as observed earlier, respond to this challenge by simply adding new ideas to the old framework. Nor can we just excise the old ideas and replace them with new ones. They are too deeply entrenched in our thinking. We need to "deconstruct" our existing ideas of knowledge (see Chapter 4), so that we can determine what we should keep and where we should go from here. Deconstructionists argue that studying patterns allows us to see below the surface to the deeper meaning systems that structure our culture. This process allows us to see how apparently ordinary ideas can constrain our thinking, undercut our wider goals and produce completely unintended effects. Deconstruction's purpose is thus to produce change. However, unlike some other forms of radical thought, it does not aim to destroy or overthrow oppressive ideas. Rather its aim is to expose the conceptual systems that produced those ideas.

ACADEMIC VERSUS APPLIED KNOWLEDGE

Within the context of this chapter, if we use deconstruction to look at how academic and vocational or applied forms of knowledge work in the educational meaning system, we can immediately see that academic knowledge is accorded the higher value. Academic knowledge is authoritative, objective, and universal knowledge. It is abstract, rigorous, timeless—and difficult. It is knowledge that goes beyond the everyday here-and-now knowledge of everyday experience to a higher plane of understanding. It is generated through brain work, by thinking hard in ways that follow the rules of reason, logic, and rationality. Although this activity happens in the minds of real people, the use of these rules somehow sets the knowledge *apart* from people: in particular, it sets it apart from the everyday desires, concerns, and feelings of the people who produced it. Thus, a school curriculum based on academic forms of knowledge must be knowledge—not student—centred: that is, its structure must follow the logic of the knowledge systems it draws from in order to imprint this logic on the minds of the students who follow it.

In contrast, applied knowledge is practical knowledge that is produced by putting academic knowledge into practice. It is gained through experience, by trying things out until they work in real-world situations. Sometimes it involves following rules and sometimes it doesn't. It is knowledge developed by people in response to specific local and/or everyday problems. It embodies people's desires, concerns, and feelings. It is usually context dependent and/or situation specific, and it is associated more with the body and physical work than with the mind. Because applied knowledge centres on people and their needs, a curriculum based on applied forms of knowledge is likely to be designed to meet the needs of the people who follow it. Applied knowledge is thus everything that academic knowledge isn't. It has looser boundaries and is less highly valued. However, the existence of applied knowledge is absolutely essential to academic knowledge because, by being what it is not, it defines it, and allows it to continue to be the higher value term.

The opposition between these two terms has, in the context of the public education system, been both a problem and a very clever means of resolving an irreconcilable conflict. As we saw in Chapter 3, an industrial-age education system needs to be able to sort people according to their likely employment destinations, and the traditional academic curriculum proved to be a useful tool for doing this. The academic-applied opposition flourished in this context and, although there have been major developments in knowledge and major changes in our education system over the last 50 years or so, it continues to underpin our thinking. Some will say that the split disappeared when most schools abolished the practice of streaming students into different courses, or, more recently, when schools began to encourage students to mix and match subjects from a range of different disciplinary areas. I don't think it has disappeared, and as one small piece of evidence for this I want to briefly describe some of the findings of a study being done by some of my colleagues.

THE "LEARNING CURVES" RESEARCH: WHAT IT TELLS US ABOUT THE ACADEMIC/APPLIED SPLIT

The Learning Curves research project is tracking the shifts in student subject-choice patterns that are occurring as the new National Certificate of Educational Achievement (NCEA) is implemented. In theory, the NCEA, along with the other changes to the organisation and assessment of student work at senior secondary school level that preceded it, has ended the old distinction between academic and non-academic subjects and offers the opportunity to accommodate a wider range of student learning needs. However, the Learning Curves research shows that the traditional discipline-based courses (such as mathematics, physics, and history) continue to be very strongly separated from the more contextually-focused or applied courses (home economics, photography, environmental education, journalism, and so on). In the schools being studied, contextually-focused courses are explicitly oriented towards meeting the needs of the learners, while the traditional discipline-based courses are strongly oriented towards meeting the needs of the discipline.

The contextually-focused courses emphasise skills and doing. Their aim is to help learners make links between school and their everyday lives, their future employment, and/or their leisure activities. These courses are being assessed internally, using mixtures of unit standards and achievement standards drawn from different curriculum areas. Some environmental education courses are using standards taken from science and social studies, for example, while some home economics courses are using achievement standards developed for use in the health curriculum area and unit standards from industry sources.

The discipline-based courses, on the other hand, continue to emphasise mastering abstract knowledge for its own sake. Teachers of these courses see themselves as having less freedom to meet the needs of their students, because learners are being assessed using achievement standards that, in many cases, involve external examinations. This, it seems, is because of a concern to maintain traditional standards and rigour, and national examinations are seen as the best way of achieving this. These courses are not using mixtures of achievement standards, but are designed around the full package of standards developed for that subject at that level. There is a strong focus on covering all the material that would have been covered in the old School Certificate, Sixth Form Certificate, or University Bursary courses. Schools do not appear to be designing courses that, through their pacing and conceptual progression, produce deep understanding of the material, or meet the needs of a specific group of students. Thus, the traditional discipline-based courses are still strongly discipline centred.

In the schools the researchers worked in, the traditional discipline-based courses have more status than the contextually-focused courses. They are seen as being harder, and as being important and necessary for those destined for professional and/or managerial forms of employment. Schools do not seem to be developing new courses that mix material from the traditional academic subjects with material from the applied subjects (although this is clearly now possible). Some teachers see attempts to intellectualise applied knowledge as a problem, while other teachers say that the changes of the last few years have diluted the traditional academic subjects to the point where students don't "get enough" of a subject to see the "the point" of it—its big picture, or overall conceptual framework.

This research is interesting because it appears that schools and teachers are not taking up the opportunities that are now available to them to put academic and non-academic forms of knowledge together. In many cases, they are actively resisting this possibility. It is clear that academic knowledge is still widely seen as *the* category—as more difficult, more rigorous, and more disciplined than other kinds of knowledge, and that the division between academic and applied forms of knowledge is entirely natural, right, and proper. However, as I have been arguing here, this idea is now out of date. The conditions under which this idea could be justified no longer apply and, if it continues to inform the way people think about the senior secondary school curriculum, schools will not be able to do a good job of preparing people for life in the knowledge society. It seems clear to me that we need to untangle some of the assumptions that underpin this idea.

BACK TO DECONSTRUCTION: TAKE I

Deconstructionists aim to show how a high-value term achieves this status. They take apart the surface-level ideas that are put forward to justify the term's status, and look for the (usually unacknowledged) assumptions that drive these. They then explore these deeper level ideas, with the aim of establishing whether they do in fact support the term's higher status (and the opposing term's lower status). If they don't, as is often the case, it then becomes possible to begin to treat the two terms as discrete and different entities that can be equally valued. Moreover, if the two terms no longer have to be treated as binary opposites, then people or things no longer have to fit into one or the other of them. Instead, they can, where appropriate, be in both. Similarly, where appropriate, the two categories do not have to be split, but can be put back together. Deconstructing things allows us to break free of the constraints of our relational, binary system of achieving meaning via a series of apparently opposite, but differently valued, terms. It is almost always a political act because, deconstructionists say, the process of undermining the basis on which one half of a binary can claim to be better or purer than the other half is, on its own, enough to produce change.

So applying this idea to the academic/applied split, what underlies the widely held belief that academic forms of knowledge are better than applied forms? How is this belief defended? What trade-offs are involved in defending academic knowledge in this way?

WHY IS ACADEMIC KNOWLEDGE HIGH-STATUS KNOWLEDGE?

Educators will give many reasons why the academic subjects have more status than the applied ones. They might say it is because these subjects are based on older established and more authoritative knowledge, knowledge that has stood the test of time and been handed down through many generations. They might say these subjects involve the kind of knowledge that an educated person needs to know, or that they are necessary for middle-class jobs and participation in middle-class cultural life. Some might say that they develop people's capacity to think abstractly, that is, beyond the here and now. Others might say that they set certain standards to be aspired to, that they are harder or more rigorous because they offer deeper and more far-reaching explanations of how the world works, and so are more powerful.

In philosophical terms, the knowledge that underpins the traditional academic subjects is powerful knowledge because it is objective: that is, it is produced by following rules that ensure that it is not contaminated by the bodily desires and concerns of the people who worked on it. It is knowledge that goes above and beyond individual people and their flaws, and above and beyond the everyday here and now. It is nonpartisan, value free, timeless, and universal: it applies to everyone and everything in all contexts. Because it is everyone's knowledge, and because it is powerful knowledge, it is supposed to play an important role in ridding the world of oppression.

Thus, the higher status of academic forms of knowledge is defended mainly on the grounds that it is *objective* knowledge. Its status depends on its ability to *leave people out*. It is for this reason that the defenders of the traditional academic curriculum will always oppose attempts to develop curricula that are more inclusive, that is, more accessible or relevant to a wider range of people. These approaches usually involve trying to put the people *back in*—a strategy that, if successful, weakens academic knowledge's high-value status.

BUT WHAT'S WRONG WITH THIS?

As we saw in Chapter 3, the scholastic specialisation arising out of streaming secondary schools students in terms of academic and applied forms of knowledge, led, in the 1940s, to the government introducing a core curriculum in an attempt to make sure all students received a "broad and balanced" general education. However, these reforms failed to change the widely held idea that the academic subjects were somehow better than the practical subjects. Things continued much as they had always been. Those who were "up to it" took the academic subjects (and learned to leave people out), and those who weren't (or who found this approach unappealing) didn't.

Later, in the 1970s and '80s, a new tack was tried. A group of social theorists (mostly British) began to publish work that strongly challenged the basis of *all* curriculum development. These writers, who came to be known as the "new" sociologists of education, pointed out that the school curriculum is a selection from all the knowledge that is available. It is a selection that reflects (and serves) the interests of particular social groups and, because of this, the school curriculum is very effective in reproducing existing social inequities rather than ending oppression (as it is supposed to). This work paved the way for the development of what became a significant movement for change in education. Many people began to argue that the school curriculum was elitist, conservative, and incapable of meeting the needs of the vast majority of the population. So far, this was nothing new. What was new was the argument that the curriculum is elitist because it uses the knowledge system of one social group and assumes that this knowledge is knowledge *per se*. In other words, it is the only viable form of knowledge. People began to advocate the inclusion of other forms of knowledge in the school curriculum—Māori knowledge, women's knowledge, the knowledge of working-class people, and so on. These forms of knowledge, they argued, are as good as those that have traditionally been included. Moreover, and most importantly, these knowledges give people from these other social groups a sense of identity, a place to stand at school, and, following from this, a greater chance of succeeding at school.

Efforts were made, in New Zealand and many other countries, to put these ideas into practice. However, as we might have predicted, when curriculum developers attempted to add elements from these other forms of knowledge to the subjects of the traditional academic curriculum, there was trouble. The curriculum developers were accused of trying to "dumb down" the curriculum. The new curriculum would produce a "lowering of standards" and a "loss of rigour". The New Zealand education system, it was argued, was "going off the rails". It was being "feminised", made "mediocre", turned into a "sea of pink fluff". The reasons for this resistance should by now be obvious.

But wait a minute. Aren't public education systems supposed to meet the needs of *everyone*? If they are, then what's wrong with these well-intentioned attempts to improve the system's ability to offer civilisation's best and greatest knowledge to everyone?

There is a problem here—and it's quite a difficult one. However, it's a problem that we have to try to solve. It's been there a long time (and many people have tried to solve it) but the need to solve it is now pressing. We must solve it if we are to make sure that everyone has what they need to participate in the knowledge age. We can no longer tolerate a system that, because it is designed to meet the knowledge needs of an élite, allows so many people to "fail". On the other hand, however, if we are to meet people's knowledge needs, we cannot simply abandon notions like rigour and standards.

The problem I am alluding to here has to do with what philosophers call relativism. Philosophers use this term to refer to the problem of what to do in a situation where different forms of knowledge exist alongside each other and there is no objective standard, or set of rules, for determining the value or quality of this knowledge. The merits of each form of knowledge can be compared *in relation* to each other—this form is better than that form. But because they have developed in different contexts, probably with different value systems, this not especially helpful; it is like comparing apples with oranges. Fairly comparing these different forms of knowledge needs an evaluation system that is external to the different knowledge systems.

When we apply this thinking to the problem of developing a national school curriculum that inserts elements taken from other knowledge systems into the traditional academic subjects, a number of questions arise that curriculum developers are not well equipped to deal with. If the subjects of the traditional academic curriculum are *not* the only possible basis for a national curriculum, then how are do we decide what *is* to be included? If every social group has its own knowledge system, and if all of these different knowledges are equally valuable, how then are we to decide who should learn which forms of knowledge? Should everyone learn the knowledge of all social groups, or should learners only be exposed to the knowledge of their social group? Is there anything that everyone should learn? If so, how should we decide what this is? Are some forms of knowledge good and others less good, or can knowledge only be judged from the standpoint of its knowers?

These are important questions. However, we have no way of deciding how to answer them from within our current frameworks. If we claim that one form of knowledge is more important or better than all the others, and, because of this, everyone should learn it, all other forms of knowledge (and, by implication, their knowers) are rendered unimportant and/or not valuable. This is clearly false. Alternatively, we can say that because all forms of knowledge are equally valuable, everyone should learn all of them. This would be to miss the whole point of the traditional liberal education, where the goal is not to simply accumulate knowledge for its own sake, but to develop the mind by exposing it to civilisation's best and greatest knowledge. A third alternative might be to say that people should learn only the knowledges that are associated with the social group they are part of. This would constrain people from participating in the world outside their immediate social group and probably disadvantage them economically. People need a sense of belonging and an identity they can be proud of. However, they also need more knowledge than can be provided by their immediate social group. They need knowledge that gives them a sense of where the wider society they are part of has come from, where it could go, and how they could contribute to maintaining what is good in it and transforming what is not so good.

The first of these three options involves excluding some people's knowledge and, by implication, those people. The second and third options involve abandoning the possibility that some forms of knowledge are better or more useful than others and, by implication, the ideal of liberal education. We are led away from knowledge as a thing in itself to a focus on the *knowers* of that knowledge. In the current system, we have to make a choice. We have to choose between relativism and excluding people. As I hope I have made clear, both of these options have major disadvantages. I think we can get around this problem, but only if educators have a wider and more open view of knowledge than might once have been necessary. This view will require them to focus on different aspects of knowledge, at a higher level, and to reframe their ways of presenting knowledge to students.

BACK TO DECONSTRUCTION: TAKE II

I have been arguing that academic knowledge is high status knowledge because it is objective: it is knowledge that rises above, and leaves out, people and their everyday concerns. However, when this kind of knowledge is the basis of a school curriculum that is supposed to meet the needs of everyone, this leaving out is a problem. But are academic forms of knowledge *really* objective? Can the basis of their claim to higher status be justified? There are good grounds for saying that they aren't, and it can't.

The last 30 years or so have seen the development of what is now a huge research literature in an area broadly known as the social studies of science. Some of this work is theoretical and philosophical, and some is based on empirical research that has followed what scientists actually do when they are researching something. I don't have the space here—and it wouldn't be appropriate—to recapitulate this entire literature, but, very briefly, it convincingly shows that scientific objectivity is an illusion. One writer calls it an "elaborate fantasy"; another calls it a "god-trick", saying that scientific method is more a rhetorical device used when writing papers reporting the findings of a research project than a set of procedures followed when actually doing the research. The empirical work shows that the values, political beliefs, everyday concerns, and feelings of scientists (and those around them) are very important in their work. They give it meaning and direction, and eventually form part of the finished work. Some of the more theoretical work has shown how the scientist (like the individual of modern political thought) is a person, but not all people can be scientists. For example, women, in the past, simply could not be scientists. Now in theory they can, but first they have to stop thinking like a woman: that is, they have to give up aspects of their womanhood. Similarly, Māori can, in theory, be scientists, but they first have to give up their Māori side. Thus a scientist's objectivity is achieved by being (or pretending to be) a particular category of person, a process that necessarily involves leaving out the other categories of person. Most of the work described here focuses on science, possibly because it is widely regarded as the epitome of objective knowledge. However, there is a smaller literature that looks at what researchers actually do in other disciplines as opposed to what they say they do (for some of the key studies in this field, see the notes at the end of this chapter).

If we accept this work, what does it mean for the status of science and the other traditional disciplines? I think it means that the higher status of these forms of knowledge *relative to other forms of knowledge* can no longer be defended on the grounds that they—and *only* they—are objective. However, it doesn't mean that science, or other academic knowledge, is no longer good knowledge. To say this would be to regress to the same old debates we need to escape from. What it does tell us, however, is that the theoretical frameworks we have been using to decide whether something is good knowledge are not adequate. We need a new theory of knowledge, one that allows us to decide what good knowledge is in a way that doesn't exclude people. If this theory is also capable of taking account of the new meanings of knowledge that are associated with knowledge society developments, then we might have a suitable basis on which to reframe our education system for that society.

I think that the new theories of knowledge that are emerging from the more philosophically inclined branches of the social studies of science literature are well suited to this purpose. This book isn't the appropriate place to map out these theories in detail. Rather, my goal here is to raise the issues and suggest a way forward. However, in the next section I briefly outline some of the features of these theories, in order to show how they could be useful in educational contexts.

SOCIAL THEORIES OF KNOWLEDGE

Using the findings of several detailed, long-term ethnographic studies of specific communities of practice as their starting point, researchers in the social studies of science are developing theories of knowledge that acknowledge knowledge's social character in ways that are not necessarily relativist. These theorists argue that all knowledge is socially produced and historically located. They say that true objective knowledge does not have to be outside history, or outside the social world. On the contrary, they argue, knowledge's social character is what gives it its value, truth, and objectivity. They draw on empirical studies of how scientists work to show how new scientific knowledge is produced in highly specific social networks that, over time, develop their own distinctive codes of practices, epistemic cultures, or rules of engagement. These codes are social in nature, but also internal to that particular network: that is, they are different from the kind of social relations that prevail in the world outside the network. This is an important point. It is this distinction—between the social practices that prevail inside a given community of practice and those that prevail in the world outside it—that makes it possible to argue that knowledge can be socially constructed *and* objective, robust, and so on.

Each different knowledge system is thus its own social world. It has its own forms of social organisation and distinctive codes of practice that generate its particular forms of knowledge (and the criteria by which that knowledge is judged). These codes of practice are not usually written down or explicitly taught. They are part of the discipline's tacit knowledge—the knowledge that its insiders know and use every day without necessarily being able to explicitly articulate it. Newcomers learn as they go, by example rather than direct instruction. The codes of practice are not fixed but change over time in response to changes in the discipline's internal dynamics. In recent times (the last 50 years or so, in particular), the pace of this change has, in many disciplines, accelerated enormously, with the result that newcomers can now expect to have to understand and adapt to an increasing number of new and different codes of practice during their working lifetime.

For our purposes here, these social realist theories are important because they put people back into knowledge. They allow us to see knowledge as socially constructed, not in the social world of the everyday, but in certain highly specific contexts that transcend the social origins of their knowers and ensure the robustness of the knowledge. Acknowledging knowledge's social character does not have to mean abandoning objectivity. However, it probably does mean abandoning the idea of knowledge as a finished set of known, accepted, fixed facts. It also probably means abandoning the idea of one fixed "gold standard" that can be used to judge all forms of knowledge in all contexts at all times.

Accepting all this helps us rethink how we might approach knowledge in schools. If we take a social realist approach to knowledge, then our knowledge of the codes of practice or epistemic cultures of the different disciplines will matter more than knowledge of their detailed facts. Thus, knowledge will continue to matter, but not necessarily in the same way it might have in the past. Given this, we should be presenting knowledge to students not as something monolithic, fixed and finished, but as something organic, something that is always developing and always in process. Instead of viewing it as a set of discrete disciplines, we should be presenting it as a series of systems that have particular ways of doing things (and particular strengths and weaknesses). Reframing our approach to knowledge in this way will allow us to work with students to develop the systems-level understanding, the big-picture, connected ways of thinking they will need to function effectively in the knowledge society.

Could we actually put this into practice? I think so, but only if we think past the industrial-age, production-line approaches to education that will get in the way. There are already many ideas around that we could use—the educational literature is full of them. Many of these ideas are not new, but when people have tried to make them work in industrial-age-style education, they have been diluted, subverted, or turned into meaningless slogans. In the last section of this chapter, I look briefly at two ideas that would, I think, work well to frame the new approaches to teaching and learning needed for this new approach to knowledge. These two ideas, using narratives, and critical literacy are, of course, not the only ideas we could use: they are just examples. Both are explicitly socio-cultural in focus. Both see the learner not as an autonomous independent mind but immersed in and formed by the wider social context. Both also focus on language and literacy, not as basic skills, but as the way people can enter, participate in, and change different knowledge systems, and develop a sense of identity in relation to those knowledge systems. Both see language, not simply as a coding system for representing reality, but as actively producing reality (or, more accurately, reality as we understand it). Similarly, literacy means something much more than the ability to code and decode text: it involves being able to participate in and, where necessary, change that reality.

NARRATIVE-BASED APPROACHES TO TEACHING AND LEARNING

As most people know, stories are an important focus of the early years of education. However, the importance of stories to all of us, no matter what age we are, is less widely recognised. Stories are universal in human thinking, and so important in all cultures. All cultures and nations have origin stories: stories about where their members came from, how they are related, and how they continue to be connected to one another. Local communities and individual families usually also have similar kinds of stories about themselves.

Psychologists agree that telling stories to young children is extremely important for their development. Children need to be able to tell stories about themselves, and to have those stories listened to and valued by people who are close to and important to them. Stories are an important means through which people engage with each other, first with those who are close to them and, later, with the other members of the culture or nation they have been born into, and with that culture or nation's knowledge systems. They are also extremely important in the formation of an individual's sense of identity: they create the context within which an individual develops a sense of self, a sense of their place in the world, and a sense of what their place in the world *could* be. Stories also develop an individual's capacity for imagination and creativity, the ability to imagine worlds that are very different from the one they are in right now, and the ability to imagine themselves doing and being things that are very different from their current reality. Thus, stories do not simply reflect reality: they play an active role in constructing it and in offering possibilities for transforming it.

Those who advocate using stories beyond the early years of primary education treat knowledge as a system of stories. A discipline is approached, at least initially, through the stories it tells about itself: how it came to be, how it works, why it is important, who its main characters are (now and in the past), and what kinds of people can be its main characters in the future. Like all other stories, these stories have a time sequence, a problem or issue to resolve, and a listener or intended audience. They also have characters or roles and, while this is not usually explicitly acknowledged, like all stories they have tellers who organise the elements of the story into a sequence that makes the story serve a particular purpose or produce a particular effect. Presenting disciplinary knowledge as a set of stories is a way of making this knowledge accessible.

Although disciplinary knowledge is, of course, more than just a set of stories, this approach offers learners a bridge between a way of thinking they all know and one that is—at least at first—alien. It also offers learners a space to imagine themselves as active players in this knowledge system. If the story meshes well with the other stories that are of part of their identity, they will find this relatively easy. If, however, they experience the story as sharply dissonant with their other stories, they will find it difficult to imagine themselves as players. Educators are well aware of this situation. However, treating knowledge systems as stories offers us a way to think about this alienation that doesn't focus on the deficiencies in the learner but instead pays attention to the interaction between the stories that a particular body of knowledge has to offer and other important stories in people's lives.

This approach is one of many possible ways we could put into practice the new model of knowledge described in this chapter. It would not only promote the systems-level, connected ways of thinking needed in the knowledge society, but also, and perhaps more importantly, it would engage a wider range of people in this knowledge.

The second approach to teaching and learning I want to look at also sees knowledge as a system of narratives or discourses and also focuses on change. This approach, known as critical literacy, will be familiar to language and literacy educators. However, it can, I think, be usefully applied beyond language and literacy to traditional disciplinary forms of knowledge.

CRITICAL LITERACY

Critical literacy, as opposed to the more basic or functional forms of literacy that are the focus of most national literacy developments programmes, is not a new idea. The critical literacy movement can be traced back to Paulo Freire and his work on developing literacy as a means of ending oppression in Third World countries. Very briefly, the term critical literacy is usually used to refer to a range of often very different approaches to teaching and learning that are united by a commitment to the connection between literacy and social change or social justice. For critical literacy theorists, literacy does not simply mean basic or functional literacy, that is, the ability to code and decode written words. Nor is it restricted to the activities of reading and writing, although both are acknowledged as the foundations which make higher levels of literacy possible. Two higher levels are usually identified. These are cultural literacy and critical literacy. Cultural literacy is understanding the meaning system or cultural context in which words achieve their meaning and critical literacy involves understanding the wider context in which this meaning system develops and changes—its "conditions of formation and transformation", to use Foucault's terms. Developing cultural and critical literacy also involve the development of an understanding of oneself—who one is, where one comes from, which social groups one is part of and how one is, or is not, part of different meaning systems.

Thus literacy, in this context, means something much more than the skills of reading and writing. One can be literate with respect to anything—history, art, psychology, science, mathematics, or technology, for example: that is, one can understand the "texts" of these disciplines at a functional level, but one can also understand them, in a critical or systems way, as part of a wider culture. However, most schools aim only to produce graduates who are functionally literate with respect to these things. Critical literacy theorists argue that if people are to make sense of, and actively produce, social, economic, and political life, they need higher levels of literacy.

Like narrative-based approaches, critical literacy offers a framework for teaching and learning that we could use to put into practice the new approaches to knowledge that will be necessary as we try to become a knowledge-based society. It would also promote systems-level, connected thinking, and the sense of self as an active player in knowledge that people will need in the new environment.

The New Basics project is a well-advanced attempt to put some of these ideas into practice. Part of the Queensland state education system, this project has developed what are known as "productive pedagogies"—approaches to teaching and learning that come from the critical literacy movement outlined above. These aim to give students the knowledge, skills, and discourses they need for the "new times". They aim to help students develop a critical relationship with the new web-based technologies and the new languages, knowledges, and identities associated with them. A major feature of this project is its emphasis on, and apparent success in, developing critical skills in *all* students, not just those destined for higher education. Putting this approach into practice has strongly challenged the Queensland public education system's old "message systems"—the interlocking sets of assumptions about curriculum, pedagogy, and assessment that, while they drove industrial-age schooling, are increasingly hard to defend in the new environment. Approaches like this, because they do not put the cart before the horse, as I think the focus on learning skills and school management does, are far more useful in providing us with the frameworks for change we need.

NOTES

so, what, specifically, are these people saying?

Pages **141–143**: For examples of recent work looking at the educational implications of the knowledge society, see Beare (2001, 2002), Carnoy (2000), Draves and Coates (2004), Andy Hargreaves (2004), and David Hargreaves (2003). See also Codd et al. (2001).

Pages **144–145**: Discussions of the importance of lifelong learning appear in virtually all the recently published policy-focused discussions of education's future. See, for example, Ministry of Education (1993, 2001a, 2001b, 2002a); OECD (1996, 2000), Prime Minister's Department (2002), World Bank (2003), and Commonwealth Department of Education, Training and Youth Affairs (2000) but there are many, many other examples. See Chapter 2 for an outline of how business management theorists see the knowledge society.

why the focus on learning skills will be opposed

Pages ***150–154***: Learning skills will be opposed for the same reasons that that the recommendations of, for example, the Thomas Report (Department of Education, 1944) were resisted. New Zealand's educational history, like that of many other countries, is littered with attempts at reform that failed because they did not mesh with the wider public's understanding of the issue. The Thomas Report and the earlier attempt to establish technical high schools (outlined in Chapter 3 of this book) are two much-discussed New Zealand examples. See Openshaw (1995) for more on this.

playing with knowledge: The end of discipline(s)?

Pages ***155–156***: Lyotard's discussion of performativity is in his 1984 book. *The Postmodern Condition.*

The notion of the new knowledge workers as a "cultural mass"—a group of people whose main work is to process, translate and interpret various expert knowledges for use in other communities of practice can be traced back to Daniel Bell's work in the 1970s (see Bell, 1978), while the notion that this translation and mediation will define what intellectual work *is* in the post-modern era comes from Zygmunt Bauman's books, *Legislators and Interpreters: On modernity post-modernity and intellectuals* (1987) and *Intimations of Postmodernity* (1992).

Page ***157***: The idea that thinking, investigating, and so on are tied to specific disciplines, and that they are different in each of them, is a basic tenet of the traditional liberal ideal of education. Teaching thinking and investigating is obviously important, but because they are not generalised abilities that cut across all disciplines, they have to be taught through the disciplines. See, for example, McPeck (1990). While it is possible that this idea may be abandoned in the new environment (which is what the learning skills advocates are effectively doing), if we accept that performativity and systems-level understanding will be important in this environment, then this is likely to be a mistake.

Page **159**: For accounts of what deconstruction is and what it can be used for, see Grosz (1986, 1989), Scott (2003), and Spivak (1989). See also Culler (1982) and Derrida (1976). For an account of the A/not-A (binary) system of meaning deconstructionists aim to expose, see Jay (1981).

the "Learning Curves" research: What it tells us about the academic/applied split

Pages **161–163**: The findings of the Learning Curves research so far (Hipkins and Vaughan, 2004; Hipkins, Vaughan, Beals, and Ferral, 2004) are available on the NZCER website (www.nzcer.org.nz).

back to deconstruction: Take I

Page **164**: The idea that deconstruction is, on its own, enough to produce change comes from Diana Fuss (1989).

but what's wrong with this?

Pages **166–167**: See Whitty (1985), Whitty and Young (1976), and Young (1971) for the early work by the "new" sociologists of education. See also Anyon (1980, 1981), Bernstein (1971), Bowles and Gintis (1976), and Willis (1977).

Pages **167–168**: The terms in quotation marks are taken from the following sources: Michael Matthews, in his book, *Challenging New Zealand Science Education* (1995) and a number of newspaper articles published in 1993, says that the then new school science curriculum is evidence that science education is going "off the rails", being "dumbed down" and "feminised". More recently, Martin Hames, in his 2002 book, *The Crisis in New Zealand Schools*, resuscitated the term "dumbing down" to describe the effect of the science curriculum document (p. 95). In addition, he describes the social studies curriculum document as a "sea of pink fluff" (p. 82), and claims that "mediocrity rules" in the English curriculum document (p. 99).

Page **168**: For an account of relativism, see Harre and Krausz (1996). For some of the objections to it, see Alexander (1995), Fay (1996), Gellner (1974, 1992), Moore and Muller (1999), and Moore and Young (2001). Nash (1991) is a discussion of relativism *vis-à-vis* curriculum development in the New Zealand context.

back to deconstruction: Take II

Pages **171–173**: The social studies of science is a huge field. For some of the best-known early work, see Barnes (1977), Bloor (1976, 1982), Collins (1983), Feyerabend (1975), Knorr-Cetina (1981, 1983), Latour (1987, 1988), Latour and Woolgar (1979), Mulkay (1979), Ravetz (1971/1996), Turnbull (1984), and Woolgar (1981, 1988). For more recent work, see Collins (1998), Shapin (1994), Toulmin (1999), Ward (1996), and Ziman (2000). For a very accessible summary of this body of work, see Sardar (2002). The "elaborate fantasy" quote comes from Walkerdine (1988), while "god-trick" is a term used by Donna Haraway to refer to the sleight of hand that, she argues, is the basis of objectivity (Haraway 1991, p.189). According to Haraway, science *is* rhetoric: it is a set of parables about objectivity and scientific method that are told to students. However, she says, "no practitioner of the high scientific arts would be caught dead acting on [them]" (Haraway, 1991, p. 184). The best known of the ethnographic studies of scientists' work are probably Knorr-Cetina (1981, 1999), Latour (1987, 1993), Latour and Woolgar (1979) and Traweek (1988, 1989). Collins (1998) and Toulmin (1999) contain detailed arguments for the importance of such studies. For work on how the category "scientist" excludes all those who are not also eligible for inclusion in the category "individual" (see Chapter 5), see the extensive literature on women and science (e.g., Bleier, 1991; Harding, 1986; Keller, 1985; Tuana, 1989) and also Gilbert (1997). Gilbert and Calvert (2003) show how women cannot simultaneously be "real" scientists *and* "real" women, and

McKinley (2002) explores this issue as it relates to Ma¯ori women. Walkerdine (1988, 1989) makes a similar case for women and mathematics. See also Irigaray (1985, 1993).

social theories of knowledge

Pages ***173–175***: For accounts of social realist theories of knowledge, see Alexander (1995), Bhaskar (1978, 1989), Collins (1998), Shapin (1994), Ward (1996, 1997) and Ziman (2000). For feminist defences of objectivity, see Barwell (1994), Harding (1992, 1993), and Seller (1988). Social realist theories of knowledge do not address the question of how and why a person's social origins may exclude them from full participation in that knowledge system. This is a different question, that, as I have argued elsewhere (Gilbert, 1997), can be addressed in other ways. For the present purposes, I think it is helpful to separate the question of what knowledge *is* from the question of how people might access that knowledge.

narrative-based approaches to teaching and learning

Pages ***176–178***: See Barwell (2000), Campbell (1997), and Miller (1995) for detailed discussions of the features and implications of the narrative mode of thought. Connelly and Clandinin (2000), Norris (1995), Polkinghorne (1988), and Sarbin (1986) (and a great many others) advocate the use of narrative-based research methodologies. Bruner (1986) and Egan (1986) make the case for using narrative-based approaches in education, and Gilbert (2001), Millar and Osborne (1998), Norris and Phillips (2003), Phillips and Norris (1999) and Solomon (2002) argue for their use in science teaching.

critical literacy

Pages ***179–180***: Paulo Friere's 1970 book *Pedagogy of the Oppressed* is perhaps the best-known example of his work developing literacy programmes in Third World countries. Barton (1994), Cope and Kalantsis (2000), Freebody, Muspratt and Dwyer (2001), Gee (1992, 1996, 2003), Kress (1985, 1996, 2003), Lankshear (1998a, 1998b, 1999),

Lankshear and Knobel (2003), Lankshear and Snyder (2000), Luke and Muspratt (1998), Muspratt, Luke, and Freebody (1997), New London Group (1996), and Street (1984, 1995) are some of the many published works exploring the concept of critical literacy. Critical literacy originates in the older idea of critical thinking. Critical thinking is an essential feature of the liberal ideal of education, so much so that the educated person and the critical thinker are more or less synonymous. See, for example, Ennis (1987), Fasko (2003), McPeck (1990), Norris (1992, 1995), Paul (1984), and Siegel (1980, 1988). Critical thinking is also strongly associated with literacy, in the sense that it is a way of thinking that evolved in parallel with writing. One cannot think critically—that is, think about thinking, about *representations* of things rather than just things—without also being literate (Olson, 1994). Thus, literacy is necessary for critical thinking, and the ability to think critically is an essential feature of critical literacy. Foucault's notion of a discourse's "conditions of formation" and its "conditions of transformation" is described in his 1972 book, *The Order of Things*.

Page ***180***: The technical papers describing the New Basics project, an executive summary, and some of the resources that have been developed are available on its website: www.education.qld.gov.au/corporate/newbasics. The "message systems" concept comes from Basil Bernstein's later work (see Bernstein, 1990, 1996).

CHAPTER 7

YEAH, RIGHT, BUT WHAT ARE WE GOING TO DO TOMORROW?

IN THIS BOOK, I HAVE ARGUED THAT A PARADIGM SHIFT IS taking place in the world outside education. Variously known as the knowledge society, the knowledge age, the post-industrial age, or post-modernism, this shift has major implications for what we currently do in schools. This shift in our thinking has two main parts. One is the change in knowledge's meaning; the other relates to new ways of thinking about individuality, identity, and equality. Most discussions treat these two parts separately. However, it seems to me that they are closely connected, conceptually and politically, and that both are extremely important for the future of education.

I have argued that our education system needs redeveloping if it is to respond to the challenges posed by this paradigm shift. We need new ways to think about knowledge and learning. Various people out there are working on this, and I have outlined some of their suggestions in this book.

However, a point I have stressed is that developing new models of knowledge and learning is, on its own, not enough. First, it won't meet the knowledge society's human resource needs, and second, it doesn't take account of education's links with social justice.

The knowledge society literature claims that *everyone* now needs skills that were formerly only developed in those destined for higher education—skills like critical, systems-level thinking, and the ability to use, critique, and modify a range of different discourses, for example. If this literature is right, then it is clear that we need to substantially lift our overall levels of educational achievement. (The current focus on basic literacy and numeracy, while it is a start, is not nearly ambitious enough.) We need to replace the production-line model of education with something much less linear, and we need to stop using the traditional academic curriculum as a tool for sorting people. However, even these things are still not sufficient. Something more is needed.

Since its very beginnings, public education has been strongly linked with social justice. Access to education has been a basic social right, and education is widely seen as the main way of producing equality of opportunity. Education is thus a collective good, and it is for this reason that it is taxpayer funded. However, to justify having a public education system, we need to make sure that it *does* contribute to equality of opportunity, even when, as is likely to be the case, we need to think about what this might mean in new ways. Developing new models of knowledge and learning will probably help to produce the kind of knowledge workers needed in the new economies but, on its own, this strategy will widen rather than reduce the gap between the haves and the have-nots. We need to make sure that we build everyone's capacity for thinking and learning, and we need to do this in ways that do not require people to be standardised. In this book, I have argued that if we are to do this, we need to take account of the second part of the paradigm shift.

Part of the old view of knowledge was a notion of what it meant to be a knower of that knowledge. A knower first has to be an individual, and, as I argued in Chapter 5, the modern idea of individuality did not include all categories of person. Traditionally, education's purpose was to bring out an individual's full potential. However, the advent of mass education saw many people coming into schools who, strictly speaking, we did not think of as individuals. This was a problem, and although we've made many changes to our education system in the name of social justice, it is a problem that we've never really solved. In post-modern thought, a new idea of individuality is emerging. The model that this idea encompasses rejects the universal, one-size-fits-all model in favour of one that emphasises diversity, difference, and plurality. The new individual is not a coherent, stand-alone entity, but a fragmented collection of subjectivities. Personhood is seen, not as something involving individuating and separating, but as an ongoing process that takes place in the context of relationships and connections. There is no end point—no stage when one is considered "finished". Moreover, because the process involves an infinite number of ways of getting there, it is not one we can standardise. This view of personhood is linked with new ways of thinking about equality and social justice, ways that don't require everyone to be the same but allow different ways of being.

These new ideas are obviously radically different from those we are used to, but if we are serious about meeting the requirements of the knowledge age, our education system has to take account of them. As I said in Chapter 1, many of the tools and resources we need to do this are already available; they are out there waiting to be used. What we still need, however, are new metaphors—new non-industrial-age lenses for looking at the educational landscape. Instead of seeing knowledge as an object we have to master, we need to see it as a process, something that happens in particular contexts and relationships. Instead of seeing thinking and learning as individual activities (and working together as cheating), we need to see thinking and learning as things that happen when people get together. Instead of trying to fill people up with all the knowledge they will ever need, we need to build people's ability to work with others to produce new knowledge that solves authentic real-world problems. Instead of trying to make everyone measure up to pre-set norms (that are actually only normal for a small proportion of the population), we need to encourage diversity and difference. Instead of trying to make everyone the same, we need a system that helps students move easily between different discourses, play different roles, and create and perform different identities (some of which may well be ones that no-one has thought of before).

As I also said in Chapter 1, this book's main purpose has been to focus on the big ideas. My aim has been to raise questions and provoke debate, not to provide a recipe for action. However, there is quite a jump between the rather abstract ideas I have been discussing and thinking about what we could actually *do* with all this, especially as much of what I have said involves turning many widely held assumptions on their head. In the last part of this book, I want to leave the discussion of knowledge, individuality, and so on, and try to say something about how we could begin putting some of these ideas into practice in real schools and real classrooms. I'll begin by returning to the two boys we met in Chapter 1.

BACK TO THE FUTURE JUST HAPPENED: BOYS, KNOWLEDGE, AND EDUCATION

Michael Lewis (who wrote the book the stories in Chapter 1 came from) argues that the activities of the boys he describes are evidence that we are in the middle of a knowledge revolution. For him, the boys in his stories are heroes. They are bravely going where no man has gone before, relying on no one but themselves. They don't really know what they are doing; they are making things up as they go along. The stories work well because, at a deep level, we already understand them. The genre is totally familiar to anyone brought up in Western European culture. It was through the same kind of adventurous, entrepreneurial, risk-taking, rule-breaking behaviour that the West was won and the British Empire was built. It was through this kind of behaviour that the world as we know it was "discovered", "understood", and colonised.

At one level, I think Lewis is right. The boys in his stories *are* heroes. Their activities are highly interesting because they clearly do challenge most people's understanding of what knowledge is and who can know it. The stories, as Lewis tells them, are highly effective in engaging us in thinking about the revolution in knowledge. However, what if we want to use these stories to help us think about these boys' experiences in the education system? How, if at all, had these boys' schooling prepared them for what they were doing? How could their experiences of school have been different? Does thinking about these boys' experiences help us to see what to do?

The boys in Lewis's stories were clearly not engaged in the education system. School for them was irrelevant and boring, but, most importantly from their point of view, it didn't offer them a place to be who they wanted to be. Although all of the boys that Lewis interviewed were, at the time he talked with them, still attending school, they were all but lost from the education system. Does this matter? Should we care? Was this the boys' fault (or maybe their parents' fault)? Or was it the education system's fault? As is probably obvious, I think the boys' dismissal of school tells us we have a systemic problem. If so, what should we do about it? Should we treat these boys as heroes? Should we dismantle the old education system and come up with something completely new that allows boys like these to really fly? Or do these boys need more guidance, or better discipline? Do we need to provide them with better role models, or with rules they can accept? Do we need to make more effort to channel their young masculine energy in socially acceptable directions—team sports, for example? Or should we encourage and develop this innovative behaviour in contexts that *also* allow these boys to build their ability to think and to help them to see the bigger picture of their activities—their effect on others, for example? How we answer these questions depends, I think, on what we consider education is for.

What these boys are doing is, at another level, just the 21st century version of behaviour that has long been valued in young males. It is behaviour that, if left alone and taken to its logical conclusion, would produce an everyone-for-themselves, all-against-all kind of world in which anything goes, and the only thing that matters is winning out over others. One of the goals of education has traditionally been to redirect and/or take the edge off this kind of behaviour—through sport and the competitive academic curriculum, through formal teaching (about ethics and civics, for example), and, more recently, via co-education, through the "civilising" influence of girls.

Traditionally, boys have been taught to accept authority and play by the rules, and this is supposed to prepare them for life in civilised society. Thus, we admire and encourage their rule-breaking behaviour while at the same time also trying to contain it. This is one of the tensions of education. On the one hand, education is supposed to facilitate individual development, to develop everyone's natural talents and their capacity for thinking and learning. On the other hand, it is also supposed to lay the foundations for civilised society—that is, a society that is not "a war of all against all". By developing everyone's full potential, we can all build a good life for ourselves and contribute to the greater good of the wider society. Thus, traditional boys' education aimed to allow and develop their natural tendencies, but within strongly prescribed, pre-set limits. It aimed to contain them, while at the same time building the foundations on which their latent abilities would (later) be able to flower. As we have seen, it did this via a highly structured environment that, through sport and the competitive academic curriculum, put a lot of emphasis on rules and discipline.

Recently, however, this system seems to have been working better for girls than for boys. This, I think, tells us something. Many educators have put a great deal of time and effort into discussions of how we can improve our education system to meet boys' needs. Some argue that our schools have been "feminised" to the extent that they no longer engage boys and that this is why so many boys are now "failing". Many strategies have been suggested for addressing this problem. These include developing teaching strategies that allow boys to be more physically active, developing incentives for bringing more men into teaching, providing other "positive role models", returning to the decontextualised competitive academic curriculum and national external examinations of the past, and developing school management strategies that involve strict boundaries, clear expectations, and stronger relationships with fathers. While many of these strategies, if introduced, would probably improve the education system's ability to meet some of the needs of today's boys, they do not deal with the question of why it is that girls are apparently now outperforming boys in the education system. Nor do they deal with the issues Lewis raises—about boys, education, and the knowledge revolution.

I'll come back to the question of girls' education shortly, but to deal with the boys first, the strategies suggested by the boys' education movement would probably *not* succeed in re-engaging boys like those Lewis describes. The present system doesn't meet the needs of these boys, not because it has been feminised, but because it focuses on an idealised past (rather than the future). It isn't meeting the knowledge needs of the boys Lewis talks about, but neither is it meeting the needs of other, more "ordinary" boys. *Can* boys like those Lewis describes—and all the other boys that have, for all sorts of other reasons, been lost from education—be re-engaged? I think they can, and I think it is incredibly important, not only for these boys but also for the future of education, that we find ways to do this.

Lewis's key message is that the old forms of knowledge, and the rules and forms of authority that go with them, have passed their use-by date. We can no longer treat the old knowledge as an end in itself, and, following from this, we can no longer use the old forms of authority and the old rules to contain boys. More importantly, however, we can no longer argue that learning to play by the old rules is good preparation for life in the real world beyond school. Life in the knowledge-based societies of the future requires a different kind of preparation.

At first glance, it is rather difficult to imagine what this might look like. However, if we look again at what Lewis's interviewees said, we can see that while their surface-level goals were very different, all acknowledged that their real goal was to be *recognised*. All the boys wanted to "get respect" and to "be taken seriously" by people in the "real world". Thus, underlying their apparently individualistic, egocentric, and competitive behaviour was a very basic *social* goal.

Recognising this makes it much easier to see how to meet these boys' needs *and* adequately prepare them for life in the knowledge-based societies of the future. The boys were impatient to join what they saw as the "real game in town". They did not want to wait for someone in authority to tell them when and where they could get the knowledge they needed, they did not want to wait until they had completed the proper apprenticeship, they just wanted to get on with it. Should we let them get on with it—and wait for them to fail? Should we dismiss all this as the unrealistic, grandiose fantasy world of youth? Should we make them knuckle down and do the real work that is required before one can really be an expert? Or should we encourage them (and others) to join the real game in town and to *be* real knowledge producers, but to do this in contexts that support them to add to their existing knowledge and skills, alone and in collaboration with others?

It will be obvious by now what I think. Leaving them to it would be anti-educational. Some boys would learn some interesting and useful things, and a few would probably be very successful indeed. However, as a strategy, it would contribute very little to the greater good, and would very likely detract from it. Nor do I think we should insist that they knuckle down and serve their full apprenticeship because doing that would not build the kind of knowledge-developing strategies we need in the future. Instead, we need strategies that build everyone's capacity for knowledge production.

Some of the strategies outlined in this book have the potential to do this. The idea of restructuring all school activities so that they resemble the workings of research groups (proposed by

Carl Bereiter and discussed in Chapter 4) is one example. The idea of schools as knowledge-producing rather than knowledge-consuming entities (proposed by Chris Bigum and outlined in Chapter 5) is another. Some of you will be thinking that nothing in the detail of what is proposed in these two strategies is particularly new. What *is* new in these strategies is that they draw together old ideas using a new logic, and they do this in a way that makes us see the old ideas in a new light. Both strategies shift our focus: they move us away from thinking about knowledge as an object to be mastered, a static end-in-itself, to a view of knowledge as a resource, something that people do things with, usually with other people, to solve real problems that matter to real people. Both strategies assume that, in a world where there is an over supply of information, the ability to make sense of what is available is now the scarce resource. Both assume that, in a world increasingly shaped by global influences, the production, accumulation, and dissemination of *local* knowledge will be very important. If people are to make sense of and act on these global influences, they first need to know a lot about themselves. They need to know who they are, where they come from, how they fit in, and how they can contribute to the wider context. Families, schools, and communities can all play a role in building this local knowledge, but schools can—and should—play a major role. Both strategies also shift our focus away from activities designed to reproduce existing knowledge to activities designed to generate new knowledge. And both emphasise knowledge building as a collaborative activity that necessarily involves building relationships, both within the team and outside it.

WHAT ABOUT THE GIRLS, THEN?

Those of you who have persisted this far may be wondering why I have spent so much time talking about boys. Is it only boys that are having problems? What about girls? Don't they matter too? Or are there no problems for girls in terms of how education is currently organised? I began by talking about boys because, in Lewis's stories, they are presented as heroic figures who show us that they can break the rules of the current system and be successful. The fact that they can do this, Lewis argues, is evidence that we are in the middle of a knowledge revolution. I have argued that these boys are also telling us that there is a problem with our current education system. Our schools are failing to engage these boys: however, they are also failing to prepare other more ordinary boys for life in knowledge-based societies of the future.

A couple of pages ago I referred to the fact that girls are now outperforming boys in our education system. Does this mean that girls now have equal opportunity and that girls no longer have any problems? Some say that it means that the pendulum has swung too far and our education system is now biased in favour of girls. They say that recent changes to the curriculum and methods of teaching and assessment suit girls more than boys. This, combined with the fact that there are too few male teachers, has feminised our schools to the extent that boys are no longer interested. I don't agree with these explanations. If girls are outperforming boys, this tells us something very interesting about our education system. Throughout Western European history, the capacity for reason (and therefore knowledge) has been strongly linked with masculinity. Reason and the feminine, in theory, do not go together. For this reason, if knowledge is being feminised, there will inevitably be anxiety and resistance. However, I don't think knowledge is being feminised (at least not the kinds that matter) and so, to a large extent, this anxiety is misplaced.

Why do I think this? As the British psychologist Valerie Walkerdine shows so convincingly in her work on girls and mathematics, when girls achieve highly in school this isn't seen as "real" success. When girls do well, this isn't because they have what it takes (reason): it is because they are diligent—they work hard and follow the rules. However, this kind of doing well isn't real success. Educational success means that one "has ability", that one has the capacity for reason (and that this reason has been "brought out"). Because, in Western European thought, one can't be a girl and at the same time, be rational, if a girl achieves highly, it is not because she has natural ability. It is because she has "done the donkey work", she has "learned the rules" and/or has "good computational skills". These things are not however evidence of rationality. Thus, Walkerdine argues, when girls are successful in the education system, their success is not actually the kind that matters. Because it isn't evidence of reason, it isn't real success. It is the *appearance* of reason, a kind of masquerade or illusion. (As Walkerdine points out, when boys don't achieve, usually because they haven't done the work, they are said to "have potential".)

However, there is another, quite different, reason for rejecting the overly feminised schools explanation for boys' disengagement. To say that the "failing boys" problem has something to do with girls is to miss the point. Boys are disengaging, not because of anything girls are doing, but because our education system is out of sync with the real world. The fact that girls as a group are now doing better than boys at school (and at early tertiary level) tells us that, whatever is going on in these places, it isn't the real game in town, and, at some level, boys know this. How could this be? Well, if we look at why it might be that girls are now *allowed* to "do well", we might notice that this is happening in a time of major economic change. For example, we currently celebrate the entry of large numbers of young women into what *were* the high-status professions of medicine and law. These professions require their practitioners to have a huge knowledge base (that is, knowledge defined in the old way). Women now predominate in these professions, just as their status, relative to other occupations, is diminishing. Lawyers now provide legal "services" and doctors are now health "service providers". Middle-class young women are moving into these professions at a time when middle-class young men are *not* doing so, but are instead going into the financial, investment, and IT sectors.

What this tells us is that the kind of knowledge one needs to be a doctor or lawyer is not as highly valued as it once was. Second, it tells us that the financial and IT sectors are now the real game in town; they are the new locus of reason and masculinity. These sectors have played a key role in the development of what we now call the knowledge society. In these sectors, risk taking, innovation, and breaking set behaviour is valued, as is the ability to develop just-in-time knowledge. Following rules and procedures slows a business down. It is old-fashioned, feminine and boring. Looked at in this light, girls' good performance in school and early tertiary education is not evidence of their success, in the sense this term is usually used. Their success is illusory, first, because it clearly does not confer a competitive advantage in the workplace, and second, because it leaves the traditional link between masculinity and rationality virtually untouched. However, it does allow them to continue in women's traditional role—first, as the stagehands and service providers to the real game in town, and second, as a reserve army of labour. The real—that is, masculine—game in town is now the generation of *new* knowledge. Thus, while old knowledge has, to some extent, been feminised, the new forms of knowledge are very definitely masculine.

This story of girls' recent experiences in the education system is, of course, very different from the one told by Lewis. Boys' disengagement with school tells us that there is a problem. But girls' apparent success also tells us that there is a problem. What is, at least initially, surprising is that it is the same problem. Our current school system is not meeting the knowledge needs of either boys *or* girls. It is out of sync with the real world and, despite superficial appearances, it has not solved the problem of equality of opportunity. The point of this book has been to argue that if we are to deal with the knowledge question *and* the equality of opportunity question, we need a new logic. Restructuring school activities as "research" or "knowledge building" would be a good way of re-engaging the boys Lewis describes. It would also be a good way of preparing people to be the kind of knowledge workers needed in the economies of the future.

However, as I keep saying, this strategy, on its own, is not enough. It doesn't deal with the wider social justice question, and it leaves the masculinity-rationality link unchallenged. If we focus on knowledge building alone, we will see the same old issues popping up—probably in new places, with new names, but the same old issues nevertheless. If we want to avoid this, the strategies we develop must acknowledge both parts of the new paradigm as equally important. Consider again, for the moment, the critical and multi-modal literacies and narrative-based teaching approaches for developing people's ability to read, act in, and transform discourses that were discussed in chapters 5 and 6. These strategies emphasise self-understanding, being able to work in a range of different contexts with a range of different people and working with difference. They are one way of reorganising education as a knowledge-building and an identity-building activity. However, unless we underpin these and like strategies with a new logic, a new way of thinking, nothing much will change.

In this new logic, knowledge needs to be not something we master as an end-in-itself, but something we do things with, something we use to solve real problems. There are many ways to approach a problem and many possible answers. Solving the problem is important, but in educational contexts, it is probably more important to develop people's awareness of different problem-solving processes. Because we cannot know what kinds of problems we will need to solve in the future, and what strategies we will need to solve them, it is very important to make sure that all possibilities are left open. It is for this reason that diversity, the second part of the new logic, is important. Identity, like knowledge, is not one single coherent thing. Like knowledge, it is something you do things with. It is something you learn to read, to play with, and to do differently in different contexts. There is no one single right way to be, but many. This is not a problem: on the contrary, it is an important resource. It is a strength, something to be developed and encouraged. A key feature of this new logic is thus the ability to work with difference—different ways of knowing and different ways of being.

YEAH RIGHT, BUT WHAT ABOUT REAL TEACHERS IN REAL SCHOOLS?

I know that when I was a secondary school teacher I would have read all this and thought, "This is all very interesting, but how can I, as one teacher on my own, put ideas like this into practice in my classroom?" It would have been important to me to cover the curriculum, so that my students were as well prepared as they possibly could be to sit the examinations they needed to do to get the qualifications they wanted. I would have been confident of my ability to teach the subject matter behind the curriculum, using conventional teaching methods. However, because I had not, at that stage, ever actually done any real research myself, I would not have been at all confident of my ability to help students plan and carry out a real research project on a topic they had come up with.

I would have been confident of my ability to manage one large group of students as a class, using the one-size-fits-all approach, but much less confident of my ability to manage several groups simultaneously. The students would need to work in groups with others of different abilities, levels of motivation, and self-management skills, and each group would be working on a completely different project. I would not have been confident that I had sufficient understanding of group processes to help my students work productively together as a team for long periods of time. Nor would I have been confident that I knew how to assess the quality of their work once it was finished.

In my classes, I would have had students who were studying five, six, or seven other subjects beside the one I was teaching them. I would have wondered how I could have expected them to focus on the demands of doing research in my class when they had a maths test tomorrow, and a ski trip the next week and when, every 50 minutes or so, they had to physically and mentally move on to the demands of the next class. Even if I could have thought of a way to deal with this, I would have known that the students, their parents, their future teachers in the tertiary sector, and their future employers expected me to teach them particular kinds of knowledge, in particular tried-and-true ways, because that's the way it has always been done. I would not have seen myself as someone who could challenge all that.

When I was a teacher, I, like many teachers, was very interested in new ideas and new ways of doing things. I had a great many ideas about how things could be different—and better. It was, however, very difficult to actually do anything that was very different from how things had always been done. I, like many teachers, eventually began to resign myself to the "fact" that this was just how things are, and I couldn't change anything. Given what I now know about our education system's history and the understanding I now have of why change is so difficult, the fact that I felt like this doesn't surprise me. However, I now think that there are things individual teachers can do. The changes our education system needs, if it is to remain viable, have to happen in individual classrooms, led by individual teachers. If teachers are to be able to make these changes, they need the support of their colleagues and their school's leadership. They also need the support of their school community—their students, their students' parents, and other community stakeholders—and the support of the Ministry of Education, the Education Review Office, and the New Zealand Qualifications Authority.

Just as teachers need to find new ways of thinking about knowledge and learning, so too do others in the education community. It was for this reason that I didn't write this book specifically for teachers, although of course I hope that some will read it. Achieving the shift in thinking that this book is about requires us as a country to develop a new public understanding about what we think and hope our education system can do for people. This will be a long, slow process of evolution, of small steps and ongoing discussion. Nonetheless, there are plenty of things teachers and individual schools can do *now* that will very definitely help to prepare their students for life in the knowledge society. This last section makes some suggestions, most of which, given my background, are directed at secondary school teachers. Many teachers are of course already doing many of these things. However, as outlined in Chapters 5 and 6, the *reasons* for doing these things are now very different.

WHAT TEACHERS CAN DO NOW

They can work together more

Secondary school teachers could change their work practices so they work together with other teachers in cross-disciplinary teams or syndicates, like primary school teachers do. This would allow them to combine their knowledge and skills to develop their strengths as a team and compensate for any individual areas of weakness. These teams could plan, for particular classes or whole-year groups, units of work that cover the different curriculum areas. These units could easily include an original research component wherein students combine elements from different knowledge areas to produce an innovation that illustrates or embodies the new knowledge they have developed. This could be, for example, a PowerPoint presentation, a video, a poster, a computer game, or a digital story.

They can think of new ways to timetable student activities

Secondary schools could find ways to organise their timetables so that cross-disciplinary teams of teachers can work together with one large group of students, probably two or more classes divided into smaller teams. This large group would probably need to have a variety of smaller spaces available to it nearby, presenting an issue for the school's timetabling team. For this system to work well, teachers and students would need to be timetabled to work together for at least two periods consecutively, and there would need to be systems for allowing students to go off site when required—to collect information, to visit outside experts, or to work in off-site facilities, for example.

They can develop their skills for helping students work in small groups

Some teachers in a school will be very good at helping students work together productively in groups for sustained periods on specified projects. Others will have a good understanding of different methods of assessing group performances (the teachers who coach team sports or lead musical ensembles spring to mind). The teachers in a syndicate could develop a knowledge-management strategy (see Chapter 2 for a brief outline of such a strategy) that would allow this kind of tacit knowledge to be articulated and shared within the group.

They can foreground students' real-world research projects

A small number of projects designed to engage interested students in research or other real-world activities currently exist in schools. These include the Young Enterprise scheme for senior economics students, the CREST awards scheme and the science fairs for science students, the maths Olympiads (and other mathematics competitions), the Technology Challenge, competitions (such as the Fair Go Ad Awards) for student-made television advertisements, Stage Challenge, Youth Parliament, and a number of environmental education programmes. Students usually work on these programmes in addition to their everyday classroom work. Many of these programmes could easily be redesigned to make them prominent parts of school activities, so structuring classroom learning for all students, not just the few who involve themselves in these activities as optional extras.

Schools could be production sites for quite sophisticated major projects: the Lower Hutt boys who recently designed and built a solar-powered car is an example that comes to mind, or one of the many combined art, drama, music multimedia productions that are now common in schools. What is important here, though, is that these activities need to be in the *foreground* of school activities. They also need to be *real* research—new knowledge production—not activities designed by teachers to get students to find out the facts to develop their research skills.

They can develop databases of community contacts

All teachers have networks of community contacts they use to help them do their work. For example, they might have a good relationship with the education officer at the local zoo or museum, or have a relationship with a local marae, someone on the local council, local business owners, local sports or cultural groups, or members of organisations like Rotary or Lions. Alternatively, they might know people who, through their work or a special interest, have useful specialist knowledge. They might also know people who can give them access to a cheap source of paper, wood, or some other useful resource. If teachers pooled all of these individual relationships and formalised them as part of an explicit strategy to develop the school's collective knowledge, schools would be in a better position to be part of—and to serve—their local communities.

These partnerships do not have to be, and should not be, one-way. Local councils, community organisations, and national organisations like the Royal Society could play a role in setting up partnerships between schools and, for example, local industries, research organisations, media organisations, and cultural groups. These organisations can help schools, and the schools can help these organisations. As suggested earlier in this book, schools could easily become sites for the collection, processing, and storing of important local knowledge: they could thus be important local knowledge *production* centres. To achieve support for such initiatives, schools will need well-thought out strategies for "marketing" them to their communities.

They can focus on developing systems-level understanding of their subject

Teachers could build into their units of work sections that explicitly aim to develop students' meta- or systems-level understanding of particular curriculum areas. As outlined earlier in the book, a systems-level understanding of a body of knowledge involves understanding how the body of knowledge works—both internally, on its own terms, and in relation to other bodies of knowledge —and how it fits into the wider socio-political context in which it developed. For example, science teachers interested in developing a systems-level understanding of science might develop, activities designed to explore the nature of scientific knowledge—what it is, how it is developed and how it is different from other kinds of knowledge. They might focus on science's impact on people (and people's impact on science), and the relationships between science, technology, and society. They might set tasks that involve comparing insights gained from one branch of science with those gained in another, or that involve exploring issues from the history, philosophy, or sociology of science. They might involve their students in discussion of the ethical issues raised by various new developments in science and technology, or discussions of risk management issues in science, questions like: "How do scientists know what they know?" "What are the limits of this knowledge?" "What can science *not* tell us?"

Teachers can also find ways to help students imagine themselves in new and different "subject positions". They can approach the teaching of their subject in ways that help students imagine themselves not as a spectator, an outsider looking in, but as a real practitioner of that subject. To do this, teachers need to emphasise, not the subject matter of, say, science, history, and art, but how a scientist, a historian, or an artist might see or think about things. They need to design activities that allow students to imagine themselves being a scientist, a historian, or an artist, and that scaffold scientific, historical, or artistic ways of thinking. Students need activities that get them to look at the rules of the game of each of these different ways of thinking—activities that get them to compare and contrast these approaches, and to look at the strengths, weaknesses, and different uses of each.

If students are to be innovators, they need to be confident users of old knowledge. They also need to be able to visualise themselves as the kind of people who can put elements from different old knowledge systems together in new ways to make new knowledge. Most people will need support to imagine themselves this way. Schools, as currently set up, do not usually provide this kind of support. However, if they are to play a role in developing the innovators of the future, then they need to be able to do this.

CONCLUSION

The task of reframing our education system to successfully prepare our young people for life in the knowledge society is indeed a significant one, as it will involve radical change, but this does not mean a wholesale rejection of everything we do now. On the contrary, we can probably most helpfully think of the task as a slight shift in focus, as using a new lens that will bring into clear view some new and different aspects of the educational landscape, allowing other aspects that currently receive considerable attention to recede into the background. Also, we already have in the educational literature many possible answers to the questions we face. What is important to acknowledge, however, is that there is no one single right answer to these questions. Nor is there a simple, one-size-fits-all quick fix. These are industrial-age ideas. Schools are not machines that need fixing because they have broken down. Rather, we can more usefully think of schools for the knowledge age as organic systems that, in the context of a clear understanding of what it is they are trying to achieve, will constantly evolve, experiment, evaluate, and change what they do to reach that goal.

For a number of reasons, it has been very difficult for schools or teachers to be genuinely innovative. First, where there are nationally mandated guidelines—for curriculum, assessment, and so on—schools can't easily do anything that doesn't fit with these guidelines. Second, industrial-age schools are specialist entities run by experts and so are necessarily distinct from other community activities. And because they are run by experts, the community tends to leave them to get on with it. As a result, most schools, while they may be the site of many community activities, are not well set up to engage with, or contribute to, whatever is really going on in their communities. Schools accordingly are not especially well set up for democratic discussion of their activities, and because the community generally knows little about the ideas that underpin their activities, they find it difficult to market new ways of doing things. Third, because our schools are so deeply immersed in the industrial-age ideas of knowledge and learning, innovative ideas tend to be reconfigured to fit these ideas, and eventually diluted to the point of meaninglessness.

It is widely believed by those who write about these things that major innovations only really occur where there is a need for, and a simultaneous coming together of, a range of different component innovations. In this kind of situation, "ensembles" of new ideas and approaches tend to develop. Some are taken up, while others are ignored. The reason why one particular ensemble is preferred over another is not always obvious at the time. It usually turns out to be the result of some highly specific combination of contextual factors that could not have been predicted. I think our schools (and our other educational institutions) are now in this kind of situation. There is a pressing need for change. The industrial-age model is under considerable stress. We no longer need the knowledge, skills, and dispositions our schools are set up to provide. There are very few jobs for the educational production line's rejects, and it is now obvious that the equal opportunity this system was supposed to provide is a myth. Schools are no longer people's main source of knowledge, and teachers are not the important authority figures they once were. Teachers, like many other professional groups, are now service providers (and it is now common for the consumers of these services to question their quality). At the same time, we have available many new and very different ideas on how to go forward. We should take the opportunity that is presented to us. We should not only use these ideas to rebuild our education system for the new era, but also use them to do some of the things we have always tried to do but that actually aren't possible in the production-line system.

It is highly likely that the innovations that arise out of this opportunity will produce schools that are organised in new and different ways. For example, it is highly unlikely that we will retain the present year-by-year progression model. It seems likely that the physical layout and location of schools will change, as will our ideas about timetabling, assessment, and the school year. We will probably see the replacement of the one-size-fits-all model of education with educational programmes or "portfolios" customised to fit the individual needs of each and every student. We will probably also see the development of specialist schools that focus on the needs and interests of particular niche markets.

Many schools and teachers are already doing these things. There are larger pockets of innovation in many places around the country, and many road maps for organising the schools of the future are already available. These more practical consequences of knowledge-society developments have not, however, been my main concern in this book. As I argued earlier, focusing on these things first is to put the cart before the horse. This book's purpose has been to make the case for change at the *conceptual* level. Only when developments to our education system are underpinned by new mental models, will we be successful in moving our schools into the knowledge age.

NOTES

back to The Future Just Happened: boys, knowledge, and education

Pages ***191–195***: Boys' education has been a hot topic among New Zealand educators and in our media for a few years now. The argument that the problem of boys' underachievement has been brought about by the increasing "feminisation" of school culture is made, for example, by Harker and Nash (1998). They say that the shift towards more internal assessment has disadvantaged boys. The levels of diligence—the continuous work patterns, the time management skills, and the rule-following behaviour—now required in schools mediate educational performance in favour of girls. Also, they say, the recent shifts in the content and emphasis of some curriculum areas have made them "just a little bit more friendly towards girls—fractionally less abstract". Fergusson and Horwood (1997) make a similar argument. There have been many articles in the popular media on this theme, and Celia Lashlie's Good Man project has received wide media coverage. In New Zealand, we have recently (July, 2004) had a major conference on boys' education (at Massey University's Albany campus—see www.boysconference.massey.ac.nz), and there have been several similar conferences in Australia (for example, in March 2003 in Newcastle). There is also intense interest in this issue in the UK and the US (see, for example, Garbarino, 1999).

For alternative points of view on this issue, see Epstein, Elwood, Maw and Hey (1998), Rowan, Knobel, Bigum, and Lankshear (2001), Smith (2003), Weis (1990, 2003), Weis and Fine (2004), and Yates (1997). Draves and Coates (2004) also argue that schools are the problem, not boys. They say that, despite the evidence of educational statistics, boys aren't behind, they're ahead. Boys (like the ones Lewis describes) are going ahead and developing the skills they'll need in the knowledge jobs of the future, while schools struggle on trying to prepare them for the industrial age of the past. According to Draves and Coates, the US saw a very similar pattern of boys' disengagement with education during a comparable period of great economic change (1900–1920). They argue that schools need to do far more to encourage and reward the risk-taking, innovative, technology-oriented bent of bright boys who find the current curriculum irrelevant and constricting. At the same time, however, they acknowledge that schools also need to ensure that *all* boys have the literacy, language, and social skills they need to cope in a complex society where most jobs will require far more of them than the ability to tinker with technology.

The article by Chris Bigun referred to on p. 197 is Bigun (2003).

what about the girls then?

Pages ***198–201***: See Keller (1985) or Lloyd (1993) for discussions of the historical links between rationality and masculinity (also discussed in Chapter 5). The work by Valerie Walkerdine I refer to can be found in her books, *The Mastery of Reason* (1988) and *Counting Girls Out* (1989). For an elaboration of the argument that girls' success is an illusion, see Gilbert (1999). See also Walkerdine (1997), Walkerdine and Lucey (1989), and Walkerdine, Lucey, and Melody (2001). The "reserve army of labour" concept is Karl Marx's.

yeah right, but what can classroom teachers do about all this?

What teachers can do now

Page ***206–207***: Athena Montessori School in Wellington, Unlimited Paenga Tawhiti Secondary School in Christchurch and the Base Six programme at Kuranui College in the Wairarapa are three examples of schools with programmes that allow secondary-age students to work on cross-disciplinary collaborative projects that are outside the usual timetable constraints and involve going offsite to work (but there are undoubtedly many others).

Pages **209–210**: For example, a recently developed resource for New Zealand science teachers, formally titled, *Entering the Debate on Genetic Modification by Developing a Critical Thinking Response*, but known as *Time for Critical Thought*, is designed to engage students in critical discussions of the debate surrounding the introduction of genetically modified crops. For more details, see www.nzcer.org.nz/researchprojects/Time for Critical Thought.

Many science educators are now exploring science teaching for systems-level understanding. See, for example, Barker (1997, 2004), Driver, Newton and Osborne (2000), Duschl and Osborne (2002), Matthews (1994), Millar and Osborne (1998), Monk and Osborne (1997), Newton, Driver and Osborne (1999), Osborne, Erduran, Simon, and Monk (2001), Solomon (2002), and Ward and Haigh (2000). Tyack and Cuban (1995), or Tyack and Tobin (1994).

Conclusion

Page **212**: See Fullan (1993), Sarason (1990), Senge et al. (2000), for discussions of why it has been difficult for schools to be innovative. See Hughes (1996) or Pacey (1993, 1994) for an exploration of the features of contexts where major innovation occurs.

Page **214**: For New Zealand roadmaps, see Chapter 13 in Charmaine Pountney's (2000) book, *Learning our Living*, or David Hood's (1998) *Our Secondary Schools Don't Work Any More*. For some non-New Zealand roadmaps, see Beare (2001), Bereiter (2002) or Senge et al. (2000).

REFERENCES

Alexander, J. (1995). *Fin de siècle social theory: Relativism, reduction and the problem of reason*. London: Verso.

Anchor, R. (1967). *The Enlightenment tradition*. Berkeley, CA: University of California Press.

Anderson, J. (1983). *The architecture of cognition*. Cambridge, MA: Harvard University Press.

Anyon, J. (1980). Social class and the hidden curriculum of work. *Journal of Education*, *162*(1), 67–92.

Anyon, J. (1981). Social class and school knowledge. *Curriculum Inquiry*, *11*(1), 3–42.

Anyon, J. (1997). *Ghetto schooling: A political economy of urban educational reform*. New York: Teachers College Press.

Anzualdúa, G. (1987). *Borderlands/la frontera: The new mestiza*. San Francisco, CA: Spinsters / Aunt Lute Press.

Barber, M. (1996). Creating a framework for success in urban areas. In M. Barber & R. Dann (Eds.), *Raising educational standards in inner cities* (pp. 6–23). London: Cassell.

Barker, M. (1997). History in New Zealand science education: Progress and prospects. In B. Bell & R. Baker (Eds.), *Developing the science curriculum in Aotearoa New Zealand* (pp. 187–212). Auckland: Addison Wesley Longman.

Barker, M. (2004). Spirals, shame and sainthood: More ripping yarns from science. *New Zealand Science Teacher, 106,* 6–14.

Barnes, B. (1977). *Interests and the growth of knowledge.* London: Routledge and Kegan Paul.

Barton, D. (1994). *Literacy: An introduction to the ecology of written language.* Oxford: Blackwell.

Barwell, I. (1994). Towards a defence of objectivity. In K. Lennon & M. Whitford (Eds.), *Knowing the difference: Feminist perspectives in epistemology* (pp. 79–94). London: Routledge.

Barwell, I. (2000). *Sex and stories: How storytelling makes storytellers as sexual characters, conscious observers and moral agents.* Unpublished doctoral thesis, Victoria University of Wellington.

Bauman, Z. (1987). *Legislators and interpreters: On modernity, post-modernity and intellectuals.* Ithaca, NY: Cornell University Press.

Bauman, Z. (1989). *Modernity and the Holocaust.* Cambridge, UK: Polity Press.

Bauman, Z. (1992). *Intimations of postmodernity.* London: Routledge.

Beare, H. (2001). *Creating the future school.* London: Routledge.

Beare, H. (2002). *Towards a learning community.* Keynote address to the Vision 2020: Technology Colleges Trust Second International Online Conference. Retrieved 13 February 2004 from www.cybertext.net.au/tct2002/keynote/printable/beare%20-%20printable.htm

Beare, H., & Slaughter, R. (1993). *Education for the twenty-first century.* London: Routledge.

Beeby, C. E. (1986). Introduction. In W. Renwick (Ed.), *Moving targets: Six essays on educational policy* (pp. *xi–xlv*). Wellington: New Zealand Council for Educational Research.

Bell, D. (1973). *The coming of post-industrial society: A venture in social forecasting.* New York: Basic Books.

Bell, D. (1978). *The cultural contradictions of capitalism.* New York: Basic Books.

Bereiter, C. (1994). Constructivism, socioculturalism and Popper's world 3. *Educational Researcher, 23,* 21–23.

Bereiter, C. (2002). *Education and mind in the knowledge age.* Mahwah, NJ: Lawrence Erlbaum.

Bereiter, C., & Scardamalia, M. (1993). *Surpassing ourselves: An inquiry into the nature and implications of expertise.* Chicago, IL: Open Court.

Bernstein, B. (1971). On the classification and framing of educational knowledge. In B. Bernstein (Ed.), *Class, codes and control* (Vol. 1, pp. 227–256). London: Routledge and Kegan Paul.

Bernstein B. (1977). *Class, codes and control* (Vol. 3). London: Routledge and Kegan Paul.

Bernstein, B. (1990). *The structuring of pedagogic discourse.* London: Routledge and Kegan Paul.

Bernstein B. (1996). *Pedagogy, symbolic control and identity: Theory, research, critique.* London: Taylor and Francis.

Bhabha, H. (1984). The other question: The stereotype and colonial discourse. *Screen, 24,* 18–36.

Bhabha, H. (1990). The third space. In J. Rutherford (Ed.), *Identity* (pp. 207–221). London: Lawrence & Wishart.

Bhabha, H. (1996). Cultures in-between. In S. Hall & P. du Gay (Eds.), *Questions of cultural identity* (pp. 53–60). London: Sage.

Bhaskar, R. (1978). *A realist theory of science.* Brighton: Harvester Wheatsheaf.

Bhaskar, R. (1989). *Reclaiming reality: A critical introduction to contemporary philosophy.* London: Verso.

Bigum, C. (2003). The knowledge-producing school: Moving away from the work of finding educational problems for which computers are solutions. *Computers in New Zealand Schools, 15*(2), 22–26.

Bishop, R., Berryman, M., Glynn, T., McKinley, E., Devine, N., & Richardson, C. (2001). *The experiences of Māori children in the Year 9 and 10 classroom: Part one—The scoping exercise.* Wellington: Ministry of Education.

Bishop, R., & Glynn, T. (1999). *Culture counts: Changing power relations in education*. Palmerston North: Dunmore Press.

Bishop R., & Glynn, T. (2000). Achieving cultural integrity within education in New Zealand. In K. Cushner (Ed.), *International perspectives on intercultural education* (pp. 38–70). Mahwah, NJ: Lawrence Erlbaum.

Blair, M., & Holland, J. (Eds.). (1995). *Identity and diversity*. Clevedon, UK: Multilingual Matters.

Bleier, R. (Ed.). (1991). *Feminist approaches to science*. New York: Teachers College Press.

Bloor, D. (1976). *Knowledge and social imagery*. London: Routledge and Kegan Paul.

Bloor, D. (1982). Durkheim and Mauss revisited: Classification and the sociology of knowledge. *Studies in the History and Philosophy of Science, 13*, 267–297.

Bourdieu, P. (1971). Systems of education and systems of thought. In M. F. D. Young (Ed.), *Knowledge and control: New directions in the sociology of education* (pp. 189–207). London: Collier Macmillan.

Bourdieu, P. (1973). Cultural reproduction and social reproduction. In R. Brown (Ed.), *Knowledge, education and social change* (pp. 71–112). London: Tavistock.

Bourdieu, P. (1974). The school as a conservative force: Scholastic and cultural inequalities. In J. Eggleston (Ed.), *Contemporary research in the sociology of education* (pp. 32–46). London: Methuen.

Bowles, H., & Gintis, S. (1976). *Schooling in capitalist America: Educational reform and the contradictions of economic life*. New York: Basic Books.

Brah, A. (1996). *Cartographies of diaspora: Contesting identities*. London: Routledge.

Brodribb, S. (1992). *Nothing mat(t)ers: A feminist critique of postmodernism*. Melbourne, VA: Spinifex.

Brown, A., Ash, D., Rutherford, M., Nakagawa, K., Gordon, A., & Campione, J. (1993). Distributed expertise in the classroom. In G. Salomon (Ed.), *Distributed cognitions: Psychological and educational considerations* (pp. 188–228). New York: Cambridge University Press.

Brown, A., & Palincsar, A. (1989). Guided co-operative learning and individual knowledge acquisition. In L. Resnick (Ed.), *Knowing, learning and instruction: Essays in honour of Robert Glaser* (pp. 393–451). Hillsdale, NJ: Lawrence Erlbaum.

Brown, J., Collins, A., & Duguid, P. (1989). Situated cognition and the culture of learning. *Educational Researcher, 18*(1), 32–42.

Brown, J., & Duguid, P. (2000). *The social life of information*. Boston, MA: Harvard Business School Press.

Bruner, J. (1986). *Actual minds, possible worlds*. Cambridge, MA: Harvard University Press.

Burman, E. (1994). *Deconstructing developmental psychology*. London: Routledge.

Campbell, S. (1997). Women, "false memory" and personal identity. *Hypatia, 12*(2), 51–82.

Capra, F. (1983). *The turning point: Science, society and the rising culture*. London: Flamingo.

Capra, F. (1996). *The web of life: A new scientific understanding of living systems*. New York: Anchor.

Carnoy, M. (2000). *Sustaining the new economy*. New York: Harvard University Press/Russell Sage Foundation.

Cassirer, E. (1955). *The philosophy of the Enlightenment*. Boston, MA: The Beacon Press.

Castells, M. (2000). *The rise of the network society* (2nd ed.). Oxford: Blackwell.

Champy, J. (1995). *Re-engineering management: The mandate for new leadership*. New York: HarperBusiness.

Chiu, C., Hong, Y., & Dweck, C. (1994). Toward an integrative model of personality and intelligence: A general framework and some preliminary steps. In R. Sternberg & P. Ruzgis (Eds.), *Personality and intelligence* (pp. 104–134). Cambridge, UK: Cambridge University Press.

Claxton, G. (1999). *Wise up: Learning to live the learning life*. London: Bloomsbury.

Claxton, G. (2002). *Building learning power: How to help young people become better learners*. Bristol, UK: TLO Ltd.

Claxton, G. (2004). Mathematics and the mind gym: How subject teaching develops a learning mentality. *For the learning of mathematics, 24*(2), 27–32.

Collins, H. (1983). An empirical-relativist programme in the sociology of scientific knowledge. In K. Knorr-Cetina & M. Mulkay (Eds.), *Science observed: Perspectives in the social study of science* (pp. 85–114). London: Sage.

Collins, R. (1998). *The sociology of philosophies: A global theory of intellectual change*. Cambridge, MA: Harvard University Press.

Connell, R., Ashenden, D., Kessler, S., & Dowsett, G. (1982). *Making the difference: Schools, families and social division*. London: Allen and Unwin.

Connelly, F., & Clandinin, J. (2000). *Narrative inquiry: Experience and story in qualitative research*. San Francisco, CA: Jossey Bass.

Cook, L. (2000). *Looking past the 20th century: A selection of long-term statistical trends that influence and shape public policy in New Zealand*. Wellington: Statistics New Zealand. Retrieved 18 May 2005 from http://www.stats.govt.nz/looking-past-20th-century/default.htm

Cope, B., & Kalantzis, M. (Eds.). (2000). *Multiliteracies: Literacy learning and the design of social futures*. London: Routledge.

Cuban, L. (2001). *Oversold and underused: Computers in the classroom*. Cambridge, MA: Harvard University Press.

Culler, J. (1982). *On deconstruction: Theory and criticism after structuralism*. Ithaca, NY: Cornell University Press.

Davies, P. (1983). *God and the new physics*. Harmondsworth: Penguin.

Davies, P. (Ed.). (1989). *The new physics*. Cambridge, UK: Cambridge University Press.

Davies, S. (1994). The competitive academic curriculum: A historical influence in Australia and New Zealand. In E. Hatton (Ed.), *Understanding teaching: Curriculum and the social context of schooling*. Sydney, NSW: Harcourt Brace.

Dawkins, R. (1998). Postmodernism disrobed. *Nature, 394*, 141–143.

Department of Education. (1944). *The post-primary school curriculum: Report of the committee appointed by the Minister of Education in November 1942*. Wellington: Author.

Department of Education. (1985). *The curriculum review: Report of the committee to review the curriculum for schools*. Wellington: Author.

Department of Education. (1988a). *Administering for excellence*. Wellington: Author.

Department of Education. (1988b). *Tomorrow's schools: The reform of education administration in New Zealand*. Wellington: Author.

Derrida, J. (1976). *Of grammatology*. Baltimore, MD: Johns Hopkins University Press.

Devine, N. (2003). Pedagogy and subjectivity: Creating our own students. *Waikato Journal of Education/Te Hautaka Matauranga o Waikato, 9*, 29–37.

Dewey, J. (1938). *Experience and education*. New York: Macmillan.

Dewey, J. (1963). *Democracy and education*. New York: Macmillan.

Donald, J., & Rattansi, A. (Eds.). (1992). *"Race", culture and difference*. London: Sage.

Draves, W., & Coates, J. (2004). *Nine shift: Work, life and education in the 21st century*. River Falls, WI: Learning Resources Network (LERN).

Driver, R., Newton, P., & Osborne, J. (2000). Establishing the norms of scientific argumentation in classrooms. *Science Education, 84*(3), 287–312.

Drucker, P. (1969). *The age of discontinuity: Guidelines to our changing society*. London: Heinemann.

Drucker, P. (1993). *Post-capitalist society*. New York: HarperBusiness.

Durie, M. (2003, March). *Mäori educational advancement at the interface between te ao Mäori and te ao whänui*. Paper presented at the Hui Taumata Mätauranga Tuatoru, Turangi.

Duschl, R., & Osborne, J. (2002). Supporting and promoting argumentation discourse in science education. *Studies in Science Education, 38*, 39–72.

Dyson, F. (1981). *Disturbing the universe*. London: Pan.

Egan, K. (1986). *Teaching as storytelling*. Chicago, IL: University of Chicago Press.

Egan, K. (1997). *The educated mind: How cognitive tools shape our understanding*. Chicago, IL: University of Chicago Press.

Egan, K. (2001). Why education is so difficult and contentious. *Teachers College Record, 103*(6), 923–941.

Eisenstein, Z. (1981). *The radical future of liberal feminism*. New York: Longman.

Elshtain, J. B. (1981). *Public man, private woman: Women in social and political thought*. Princeton, NJ: Princeton University Press.

Ennis, R. (1987). A taxonomy of critical thinking dispositions and abilities. In J. Baron & R. Sternberg (Eds.), *Teaching thinking skills* (pp. 9–26). New York: W. H. Freeman.

Epstein, D., Elwood, J., Maw, V., & Hey, J. (Eds.). (1998). *Failing boys? Issues in gender and achievement*. Buckingham: Open University Press.

Fasko, D. (Ed.). (2003). *Critical thinking and reasoning: Current theories, research and practice*. Cresskill, NJ: Hampton Press.

Fay, B. (1996). *Contemporary philosophy of social science*. Oxford: Blackwell.

Fergusson, D., & Horwood, J. (1997). Gender differences in educational achievement in a New Zealand birth cohort. *New Zealand Journal of Educational Studies, 32*(1), 83–96.

Feyerabend, P. (1975). *Against method*. London: Verso.

Flax, J. (1990). *Thinking fragments: Psychoanalysis, feminism, and postmodernism in the contemporary West*. Berkeley, CA: University of California Press.

Flax, J. (1992). The end of innocence. In J. Butler & J. Scott (Eds.), *Feminists theorise the political* (pp. 445–463). New York: Routledge.

Flax, J. (1993). *Disputed subjects: Essays on psychoanalysis, politics and philosophy*. New York: Routledge.

Flax, J. (1996). Taking multiplicity seriously: Some implications for psychoanalytic theorizing and practice. *Contemporary Psychoanalysis, 32*(4), 577–593.

Florida, R. (2002). *The rise of the creative class*. New York: Basic Books.

Foucault, M. (1972). *The archaeology of knowledge*. London: Routledge.

Freebody, P., Muspratt, S., & Dwyer, B. (Eds.). (2001). *Difference, silence, and textual practice: Studies in critical literacy*. Cresskill, NJ: Hampton Press.

Freire, P. (1970). *Pedagogy of the oppressed*. Harmondsworth: Penguin.

Fullan, M. (1993). *Change forces: Probing the depths of educational reform*. London: Falmer.

Fuss, D. (1989). *Essentially speaking: Feminism, nature and difference*. New York: Routledge.

Garbarino, J. (1999). *Lost boys*. New York: Anchor.

Gardner, H. (1983). *Frames of mind: The theory of multiple intelligences*. New York: Basic Books.

Gardner, H. (1985). *The mind's new science: A history of the cognitive revolution*. New York: Basic Books.

Gardner, H. (1991). *The unschooled mind: How children think and how schools should teach*. New York: Basic Books.

Gardner, H. (1999). *Intelligence re-framed: Multiple intelligences for the 21st century*. New York: Basic Books.

Gee, J. P. (1992). *The social mind: Language, ideology and social practice*. New York: Bergin & Garvey.

Gee, J. P. (1996). *Social linguistics and literacies: Ideology in discourses* (2nd ed.). London: Taylor & Francis.

Gee, J. P. (2001). Quality, science and the life world: The alignment of business and education. In P. Freebody, S. Muspratt, & B. Dwyer (Eds.), *Difference, silence, and textual practice: Studies in critical literacy* (pp. 359–382). Cresskill, NJ: Hampton Press.

Gee, J. P. (2003). *What video games have to teach us about learning and literacy*. New York: Palgrave Macmillan.

Gee, J. P., Hull, G., & Lankshear, C. (1996). *The new work order: Behind the language of the new capitalism*. Sydney, NSW: Allen and Unwin.

Gellner, E. (1974). The new idealism. In A. Giddens (Ed.), *Positivism and sociology* (pp. 129–156). London: Heinemann.

Gellner, E. (1992). *Postmodernism, reason and religion*. London: Routledge.

Gergen, K. (1991). *The saturated self: Dilemmas of identity in contemporary life*. New York: Basic Books.

Gibbons, M., Limoges, C., Nowotny, H., Schwartzman, S., Scott, P., & Trow, M. (1994). *The new production of knowledge: The dynamics of science and research in contemporary societies*. London: Sage.

Giddens, A. (1991). *Modernity and self-identity: Self and society in the late modern age*. Stanford, CA: Stanford University Press.

Giddens, A. (1998). *The third way: The renewal of social democracy*. Cambridge, UK: Polity Press.

Gilbert, J. (1997). *Thinking "other"-wise: Re-thinking the problem of girls and science education in the post-modern*. Unpublished doctoral thesis, University of Waikato, Hamilton.

Gilbert, J. (1999). "It's life, Jim, but not as we know it": The trouble with girls' achievements in science education. *Women's Studies Journal, 15*(2), 9–27.

Gilbert, J. (2001). Developing narrative-based approaches to science education: Re-thinking an "old" discipline for the "Knowledge Society". In B. Cope & M. Kalantzis (Eds.), *Learning for the future: Proceedings of the Learning Conference, 2001*. Common Ground: Melbourne.

Gilbert, J., & Calvert, S. (2003). Challenging accepted wisdom: Looking at the gender and science education question through a different lens. *International Journal of Science Education, 25*(7), 861–878.

Gilroy, P. (1993). *The Black Atlantic*. London: Verso.

Goleman, D. (1996). *Emotional intelligence: Why it can matter more than IQ*. London: Bloomsbury.

Goodson, I. (1983). Defining and defending the subject: Geography versus environmental studies. In M. Hammersley & A. Hargreaves (Eds.), *Curriculum practice: Some sociological case studies* (pp. 89–106). Lewes: Falmer Press.

Goodson, I. (1985). *Social histories of the secondary curriculum*. Lewes: Falmer Press.

Goodson, I. (1988). *The making of curriculum*. Lewes: Falmer Press.

Goodson, I. (1992). On curriculum form: Notes towards a theory of curriculum. *Sociology of Education, 65*, 66–75.

Gould, S. (1981). *The mismeasure of man*. New York: Norton.

Gramsci, A. (1971). *Selections from the prison notebooks*. London: Lawrence & Wishart.

Grossberg, L. (1996). Identity and cultural studies: Is that all there is? In S. Hall & P. du Gay (Eds.), *Questions of cultural identity* (pp. 87–107). London: Sage.

Grosz, E. (1986). Derrida, Irigaray and deconstruction. *Left-wright, Intervention, 20*, 73.

Grosz, E. (1989). *Sexual subversions: Three French feminists*. Sydney, NSW: Allen and Unwin.

Gunew, S., & Yeatman, A. (Eds.). (1993). *Feminism and the politics of difference*. Sydney, NSW: Allen & Unwin.

Gutmann, A. (1980). *Liberal equality*. Cambridge, UK: Cambridge University Press.

Hall, S. (1992). New ethnicities, In J. Donald & A. Rattansi (Eds.), *"Race", culture and difference* (pp. 252–259). London: Sage.

Hames, M. (2002). *The crisis in New Zealand schools*. Palmerston North: Dunmore Press.

Handy, C. (1989). *The age of unreason*. London: Business Books.

Handy, C. (1994). *The age of paradox*. Boston, MA: Harvard Business School Press.

Haraway, D. (1991). Situated knowledges: The science question in feminism and the privilege of partial perspective. In D. Haraway (Ed.), *Simians, cyborgs and women: The reinvention of nature* (pp. 183–201). London: Free Association Books.

Harding, S. (1986). *The science question in feminism*. Ithaca, NY: Cornell University Press.

Harding, S. (1992). After the neutrality ideal: Science, politics and "strong objectivity". *Social Research, 59*, 567–587.

Harding, S. (1993). Re-thinking standpoint epistemology: What is "strong objectivity"? In L. Alcoff & E. Potter (Eds.), *Feminist epistemologies* (pp. 49–82). New York: Routledge.

Hargreaves, A. (2004). *Teaching in the Knowledge Society*. New York: Teachers College Press.

Hargreaves, D. (2003). *Education epidemic: Transforming secondary schools through innovation networks*. London: Demos. (Available at www.demos.co.uk)

Harker, R. (1990). Schooling and cultural reproduction. In J. Codd, R. Harker, & R. Nash (Eds.), *Political issues in New Zealand education* (2nd ed., pp. 25–42). Palmerston North: Dunmore Press.

Harré, R., & Gillett, G. (1994). *The discursive mind*. Thousand Oaks, CA: Sage.

Harré, R., & Krausz, M. (1996). *Varieties of relativism*. Oxford: Blackwell.

Harvey, D. (1990). *The condition of postmodernity: An enquiry into the origins of cultural change*. Oxford: Basil Blackwell.

Hattie, J. (2003, February). *New Zealand education snapshot*. Paper presented at the Knowledge Wave 2003 Leadership Forum, Auckland.

Henriques, J., Hollway, W., Urwin, C., Venn, C., & Walkerdine, V. (Eds.). (1984). *Changing the subject: Psychology, social regulation and subjectivity*. London: Methuen.

Herrnstein, R., & Murray, C. (1994). *The Bell Curve: Intelligence and class structure in American life*. New York: Free Press.

Hipkins, R., Vaughan, K., Beals, F., & Ferral, H. (2004). *Learning curves: Shared pathways and multiple tracks: Meeting student learning needs in an evolving qualifications regime*. Wellington: New Zealand Council for Educational Research.

Hirschfeld, L., & Gelman, S. (1994). *Mapping the mind: Domain specificity in cognition and culture*. New York: Cambridge University Press.

Hirst, P. (1972). Liberal education and the nature of knowledge. In R. Dearden, P. Hirst, & R. Peters (Eds.), *Education and reason* (pp. 1–24). London: Routledge and Kegan Paul.

Hirst, P. (1974). *Knowledge and the curriculum*. London: Routledge and Kegan Paul.

Hirst, P., & Peters, R. (1970). *The logic of education*. London: Routledge and Kegan Paul.

Hood, D. (1998). *Our secondary schools don't work any more*. Auckland: Profile Books.

Horkheimer, M., & Adorno, T. (1972). *The dialectic of enlightenment*. New York: Herder and Herder.

Hughes, T. (1996). Technological momentum. In M. Smith & L. Marx (Eds.), *Does technology drive history? The dilemma of technological determinism*. Cambridge, MA: MIT Press.

HUMANZ Knowledge Policy Research Group. (2000). *Knowledge, innovation and creativity: Designing a knowledge society for a small democratic country*. Report written for the New Zealand Ministry of Research, Science and Technology. Wellington: HUMANZ.

Information Technology Advisory Group (ITAG) New Zealand. (1999). *The knowledge economy*. Wellington: Author. (Available at http://www.med.govt.nz/pbt/infotech/knowledge_economy/knowledge_economy.pdf)

Irigaray, L. (1985). *This sex which is not one*. Ithaca, NY: Cornell University Press.

Irigaray, L. (1993). *An ethics of sexual difference*. Ithaca, NY: Cornell University Press.

Jacoby, R., & Glauberman, N. (Eds.). (1995). *The Bell Curve debate*. New York: Random House.

Jagose, A. (1993). Slash and suture: Post/colonialism in borderlands/la frontera: The new mestiza. In S. Gunew & A. Yeatman (Eds.), *Feminism and the politics of difference* (pp. 212–227). Sydney: Allen & Unwin.

Jameson, F. (1991). *Postmodernism, or, the cultural logic of late capitalism*. Durham, NC: Duke University Press.

Jay, N. (1981). Gender and dichotomy. *Feminist Studies*, *7*(1), 38–56.

Jenkins, K., & Jones, A. (2000). Mäori education policy: A state promise. In J. Marshall, E. Coxon, K. Jenkins, & A. Jones (Eds.), *Politics, policy, pedagogy: Education in Aotearoa/New Zealand* (pp. 139–156). Palmerston North: Dunmore Press.

Keller, E. F. (1985). *Reflections on gender and science.* New Haven, CN: Yale University Press.

Kenway, J., & Bullen, E. (2001). *Consuming children: Education, entertainment, and advertising.* Buckingham, UK: Open University Press.

Knorr-Cetina, K. (1981). *The manufacture of knowledge.* Oxford: Pergamon Press.

Knorr-Cetina, K. (1983). The ethnographic study of scientific work: Towards a constructivist interpretation of science. In K. Knorr-Cetina & M. Mulkay (Eds.), *Science observed: Perspectives in the social study of science.* London: Sage.

Knorr-Cetina, K. (1999). *Epistemic cultures: How the sciences make knowledge.* Cambridge, MA: Harvard University Press.

Kress, G. (1985). *Linguistic processes in sociocultural practice.* Oxford: Oxford University Press.

Kress, G. (1996). *Before writing: Re-thinking paths into literacy.* London: Routledge.

Kress, G. (2003). *Literacy in the new media age.* London: Routledge.

Kuhn, T. (1970). *The structure of scientific revolutions.* Chicago, IL: Chicago University Press.

Lakoff, G. (1987). *Women, fire and dangerous things: What categories reveal about the mind.* Chicago, IL: Chicago University Press.

Lakoff, G., & Johnson, M. (1980). *Metaphors we live by.* Chicago, IL: Chicago University Press.

Landes, D. (1998). *Homo faber, Homo sapiens*: Knowledge, technology, growth and development. In D. Neef (Ed.), *The knowledge economy* (pp. 53–73). Boston, MA: Butterworth-Heinemann

Lankshear, C. (1998a). Frameworks and workframes: Evaluating literacy policy. *Unicorn, 24*(2), 43–58.

Lankshear, C. (1998b, April). *Critical literacies and the new technologies.* Paper presented at the annual meeting of the American Educational Research Association (AERA), San Diego. (Available at http://www.geocities.com/c.lankshear/work.html)

Lankshear, C. (1999). Literacy studies in education: Disciplined developments in a post-disciplinary age. In M. Peters (Ed.), *After the disciplines: The emergence of cultural studies* (pp. 199–227). Westport, CT: Bergin & Garvey,

Lankshear, C., Gee, J. P., Knobel, M., & Searle, C. (1997). *Changing literacies*. Buckingham, UK: Open University Press.

Lankshear, C., & Knobel, M. (2000). *What is digital epistemologies?* Retrieved from http://www.geocities.com/c.lankshear/work.html

Lankshear, C., & Knobel, M. (2002). Do we have your attention? New literacies, digital technologies and the education of adolescents. In D. Alvermann (Ed.), *Adolesecents and literacies in a digital world* (pp. 19–39). New York: Peter Lang.

Lankshear, C., & Knobel, M. (2003). *New literacies: Changing knowledge and classroom learning*. Buckingham, UK: Open University Press.

Lankshear, C., Peters, M., & Knobel, M. (2000). Information, knowledge and learning: Some issues facing epistemology and education in a digital age. *Journal of Philosophy of Education*, *34*(1), 17–40.

Lankshear, C., & Snyder, I. (2000). *Teachers and techno-literacy*. Sydney: Allen & Unwin.

Lash, S., & Urry, J. (1994). *Economies of signs and space*. London: Sage.

Latour, B. (1987). *Science in action: How to follow scientists and engineers through society*. Cambridge, MA: Harvard University Press.

Latour, B. (1988). *The Pasteurisation of France*. Cambridge, MA: Cambridge University Press.

Latour, B. (1993). *We have never been modern*. Hemel Hempstead: Harvester Wheatsheaf.

Latour, B., & Woolgar, S. (1979). *Laboratory life: The social construction of scientific facts*. London: Sage.

Lave, J. (1988). *Cognition in practice: Mind, mathematics and culture in everyday life*. Cambridge, MA: Cambridge University Press.

Lave, J., & Wenger, E. (1991). *Situated learning: Legitimate peripheral participation*. Cambridge, UK: Cambridge University Press.

Layton, D. (1972). Science as general education. *Trends in Education*, *25*, 11–15.

Layton, D. (1995). Constructing and reconstructing school technology in England and Wales. *International Journal of Technology and Design Education*, *5*, 89–118.

Lea, M., & Nicoll, K. (Eds.). (2002). *Distributed learning: Social and cultural approaches to practice*. London: RoutledgeFalmer.

LEK Consulting. (2001). *The New Zealand Talent Initiative: Strategies for building a talented nation*. Report to the Prime Minister, November. (Available at www.executive.govt.nz/minister/clark/innovate/index.html)

Lewis, M. (2001). *Next: The future just happened.* New York: W. W. Norton.

Lloyd, G. (1993). *The man of reason: "Male" and "female" in Western philosophy*. London: Routledge.

Locke, J. (2004, March 17–23). Taking a team approach. *Education Review*, p. 19.

Lugones, M. (1982). Playfulness, "world"-travelling and loving perception. *Hypatia*, *2*(2), 3–19.

Lugones, M. (1994). On the logic of pluralist feminism. In C. Card (Ed.), *Feminist ethics*. Lawrence, KS: Kansas University Press.

Luke, A., & Luke, C. (2000). A situated perspective on cultural globalisation. In N. Burbules & C. Torres (Eds.), *Globalisation and education: Critical perspectives* (pp. 275–297). New York: Routledge.

Luke, A., & Muspratt, S. (1998). *Constructing critical literacies*. Sydney, NSW: Allen & Unwin.

Lumby, C. (1999). *Gotcha: Life in a tabloid world*. Sydney, NSW: Allen & Unwin.

Lyotard, J. F. (1984). *The postmodern condition: A report on knowledge*. Manchester: Manchester University Press.

MacPherson, C. B. (1962). *The political theory of possessive individualism: Hobbes to Locke*. Oxford: Oxford University Press.

Margulis. L., & Sagan D. (1995). *What is life?* New York: Simon and Schuster.

Matthews, M. (1994). *Science teaching: The role of history and philosophy of science*. New York: Routledge.

Matthews, M. (1995). *Challenging New Zealand science education*. Palmerston North: Dunmore Press.

Matthews, M. (1993, 12 October). Science teaching off the rails. *The Dominion*, p. 6.

Maturana, H., & Varela, F. (1987). *The tree of knowledge: The biological roots of human understanding*. Boston, MA: New Science Library.

McCulloch, G., Jenkins, E., & Layton, D. (1985). *Technological revolution?* Lewes: Falmer Press.

McDonald, G. (1992). Are girls smarter than boys? In S. Middleton & A. Jones (Eds.), *Women and education in Aotearoa 2* (pp. 102–121). Wellington: Bridget Williams Books.

McDonald, G. (1998). Working its magic? IQ rise and the demography of the classroom. *Oxford Review of Education*, *24*(2), 225–234.

McKenzie, D. (1992). The technical curriculum: Second class knowledge? In G. McCulloch (Ed.), *The school curriculum in New Zealand: History, theory, policy and practice* (pp. 29–39). Palmerston North: Dunmore Press.

McKenzie, D., Lee, H., & Lee, G. (1996). *Scholars or dollars? Selected historical case studies of opportunity costs in New Zealand education*. Palmerston North: Dunmore Press.

McKinley, E. (2002). *Brown bodies, white coats: Post-colonialism, Mäori women and science*. Unpublished doctoral thesis, University of Waikato, Hamilton.

McPeck, J. (1990). *Teaching critical thinking*. New York: Routledge.

Millar, R., & Osborne, J. (Eds.). (1998). *Beyond 2000: Science education for the future*. London: King's College, London.

Miller, J. (1995). Narrative. In F. Lentricchia & T. McLaughlin (Eds.), *Critical terms for literary study* (pp. 66–79). Chicago, IL: University of Chicago Press.

Ministry of Education. (1993). *The New Zealand curriculum framework: Te anga marautanga o Aotearoa*. Wellington: Author/ Learning Media.

Ministry of Education. (1998). *Interactive education: An information and communication technologies strategy for schools*. Wellington: Author.

Ministry of Education. (1999). *Briefing for the incoming Minister of Education 1999*. Wellington: Author. (Available at www.minedu.govt.nz)

Ministry of Education. (2000). *Report of the compulsory schools sector in New Zealand: Nga kura o Aotearoa*. Wellington: Author.

Ministry of Education. (2001a, August). *Theme 2: People and capability*. Paper written for the Catching the Knowledge Wave conference, Auckland. (Available at http://www.knowledge wave.org.nz/conference_2001/documents/People%20and %20Capability%202.pdf)

Ministry of Education. (2001b). *New Zealand schools: Nga kura o Aotearoa* (known as the "Schools Sector" report). Wellington: Author.

Ministry of Education. (2002a). *2002 briefing for the incoming Minister of Education*. Wellington: Author. (Available at www.minedu.govt.nz)

Ministry of Education. (2002b). *Information and communication technologies strategy for schools 2002–2004*. Wellington: Author. (Available at www.minedu.govt.nz)

Monk, M., & Osborne, J. (1997). Placing the history and philosophy of science on the curriculum: A model for the development of pedagogy. *Science Education, 81*(4), 405–424.

Moore, R., & Muller, J. (1999). The discourse of "voice" and the problem of knowledge and identity in the sociology of education. *British Journal of Sociology of Education, 20*, 189–206.

Moore, R., & Young, M. (2001). Knowledge and the curriculum in the sociology of education: Towards a re-conceptualisation. *British Journal of Sociology of Education, 22*(4), 445–461.

Morris, A., & Stewart-Dore, N. (1984). *Learning to learn from text: Effective reading in the content areas*. Sydney, NSW: Addison-Wesley.

Morss, J. (1996). *Growing critical: Alternatives to developmental psychology*. London: Routledge.

Mortimore, P., & Whitty, G. (1997). *Can school improvement overcome the effects of disadvantage?* London: University of London Institute of Education.

Mulkay, M. (1979). *Science and the sociology of knowledge*. London: Allen & Unwin.

Musgrave, A. (1993). *Common sense, science and scepticism*. Cambridge, UK: Cambridge University Press.

Muspratt, S., Luke, A., & Freebody, P. (Eds.). (1997). *Constructing critical literacies: Teaching and learning textual practice*. Cresskill, NJ: Hampton Press.

Nash, R. (1986). Educational and social inequality: The theories of Bourdieu and Boudon with reference to class and ethnic differences in New Zealand. *New Zealand Sociology, 1*(2), 121–137.

Nash, R. (1991). In defence of a common curriculum and a universal pedagogy. In J. Morss & T. Linzey (Eds.), *Growing up: The politics of human learning* (pp. 210–226). Auckland: Longman Paul.

Nash, R., & Harker R. (1998). *Making progress: Adding value in secondary education*. Palmerston North: ERDC Press.

Neef, D. (Ed.). (1998). *The knowledge economy*. Boston, MA: Butterworth-Heinemann.

Negroponte, N. (1995). *Being digital*. New York: Vintage.

New London Group. (1996). A pedagogy of multiliteracies: Designing social futures. *Harvard Educational Review, 66*, 60–92.

Newton, P., Driver, R., & Osborne, J. (1999). The place of argumentation in the pedagogy of school science. *International Journal of Science Education, 21*(5), 553–576.

Norris, S. (Ed.). (1992). *The generalisability of critical thinking: Multiple perspectives on a functional ideal*. New York: Teachers College Press.

Norris, S. (1995). Sustaining and responding to charges of bias in critical thinking. *Educational Theory, 45*(2), 199–211.

Norris, S., & Phillips, L. (2003). How literacy in its descriptive sense is central to scientific literacy. *Science Education, 86*, 224–240.

Oblinger, D., & Oblinger, J. (Eds.). (2005). *Educating the net generation.* Boulder. CO: Educause. (Available at www.educause.edu/LibraryDetailPage/666?ID=PUB7101)

[OECD: see Organisation for Economic Co-operation and Development]

Olson, D. (1994). *The world on paper.* Cambridge, UK: Cambridge University Press.

Olssen, M. (Ed.). (1988). *Mental testing in New Zealand: Critical and oppositional perspectives.* Dunedin: University of Otago Press.

Openshaw, R. (1995). *Unresolved struggle: Consensus and conflict in New Zealand state post-primary education.* Palmerston North: Dunmore Press.

Openshaw, R., Lee, G., & Lee, H. (1993). *Challenging the myths: Rethinking New Zealand's educational history.* Palmerston North: Dunmore Press.

Oppenheimer, T. (2003). *The flickering mind: The false promise of technology in the classroom and how learning can be saved.* New York: Random House.

Organisation for Economic Co-operation and Development (OECD). (1996). *Education and training: Learning and working in a society in flux.* Paris: Author.

Organisation for Economic Co-operation and Development (OECD). (2000). *Knowledge management in the learning society.* Paris: Centre for Educational Research and Innovation, OECD.

Osborne, J., Erduran, S., Simon, S., & Monk, M. (2001). Enhancing the quality of argument in school science. *School Science Review, 82*(301), 63–70.

Pacey, A. (1993). *The maze of ingenuity: Ideas and idealism in the development of technology* (2nd ed.). Cambridge, MA: MIT Press.

Pacey, A. (1994). *The culture of technology.* Cambridge, MA: MIT Press.

Paechter, C. (2000). *Changing school subjects: Power, gender and curriculum.* Buckingham, UK: Open University Press.

Parker, I. (1992). *Discourse dynamics: Critical analysis for social and individual psychology*. London: Routledge.

Pateman, C. (1988). *The sexual contract*. Cambridge, UK: Polity Press.

Pateman, C. (1989). *The disorder of women: Democracy, feminism and political theory*. Cambridge, UK: Polity Press.

Paul, R. (1984). Critical thinking: Fundamental to education for a free society. *Educational Leadership, 42*(1), 14.

Penetito, W. (2002). Research and context for a theory of Māori schooling. *McGill Journal of Education, 37*(1), 89–109.

Perelman, L. (1992). *School's out: Hyperlearning, the new technology and the end of education*. New York: William Morrow.

Peters, M. (2001a). National education policy constructions of the "knowledge economy": Towards a critique. *Journal of Educational Enquiry, 2*(1), 1–22.

Peters, M. (2001b). Education policy research and the global knowledge economy. *Access: Critical Perspectives on Cultural and Policy Studies in Education*, *19*(2), 90–101.

Peters, T. (1992). *Liberation management: Necessary disorganisation for the nanosecond nineties*. New York: Fawcett.

Phillips, L., & Norris, S. (1999). Interpreting popular reports of science: What happens when the reader's world meets the world on paper? *International Journal of Science Education, 21*, 317–327.

Pinker, S. (1997). *How the mind works*. New York: Norton.

Pinker, S. (2002). *The blank slate: The modern denial of human nature*. London: Allen Lane.

Polanyi, K. (1957). *The great transformation: The political and economic origins of our time*. Boston, MA: The Beacon Press.

Polkinghorne, D. (1988). *Narrative knowing and the human sciences*. Albany, NY: State University of New York Press.

Popper, K. (1966). *The open society and its enemies: (Vol. 1) The spell of Plato* (5th ed.). London: Routledge and Kegan Paul.

Pountney, C. (2000). *Learning our living: A teaching autobiography*. Auckland: Cape Catley.

Prichard, C., Hull, R., Chumer, M., & Willmott, H. (Eds.). (2000).

Managing knowledge: Critical investigations of work and learning. London: Macmillan Business.

Prime Minister's Department. (2002). *Growing an innovative New Zealand.* Wellington: Author. (Available at www.executive.govt.nz/minister/clark/innovate/index.html)

Probst, G., Raub, S., & Romhardt, K. (2000). *Managing knowledge: Building blocks for success.* Chichester: John Wiley & Sons.

Rancière, J. (1992). Politics, identification and subjectivization. *October, 61,* 58–65.

Ravetz, J. (1996). *Scientific knowledge and its social problems* (2nd ed.). New Brunswick: Transaction.

Renwick, W. (1986). *Moving targets: Six essays on educational policy.* Wellington: New Zealand Council for Educational Research.

Rifkin, J. (1998). *The biotech century: Harnessing the gene and re-making the world.* New York: Tarcher Putnam.

Riley, D. (1988). *"Am I that name?" Feminism and the category of "women" in history.* London: Macmillan.

Rogoff, B. (1990). *Apprenticeship in thinking: Cognitive development in a social context.* Cambridge, UK: Cambridge University Press.

Rogoff, B., & Lave, J. (1984). *Everyday cognition: Development in social context.* Cambridge, MA: Harvard University Press.

Rowan, L., Knobel, M., Bigum, C., & Lankshear, C. (2001). *Boys, literacies and schooling: The dangerous territories of gender-based literacy reform.* Buckingham, UK: Open University Press.

Rumelhart, D. (1989). The architecture of mind: A connectionist approach. In M. Posner (Ed.), *Foundations of cognitive science* (pp. 133–159). Cambridge, MA: MIT Press.

Rumelhart, D., McClelland, J., & the PDP Research Group. (1986). *Parallel distributed processing: Explorations in the microstructure of cognition: (Vol. 1) Foundations.* Cambridge, MA: MIT Press.

Salomon, G. (Ed.). (1993). *Distributed cognitions: Psychological and educational considerations.* New York: Cambridge University Press.

Sarason, S. (1990). *The predictable failure of educational reform.* San Francisco, CA: Jossey Bass.

Sarbin, T. (Ed.). (1986). *Narrative psychology: The storied nature of human conduct*. New York: Praeger.

Sardar, Z. (2002). Thomas Kuhn and the science wars. In R. Appignanesi (Ed.), *Postmodernism and big science* (pp. 187–233). Cambridge, UK: Icon Books.

Sartori, D. (1994). Women's authority in science. In K. Lennon & M. Whitford (Eds.), *Knowing the difference: Feminist perspectives in epistemology* (pp. 110–121). London: Routledge.

Scheffler, I. (1965). *Conditions of knowledge*. Chicago, IL: Scott Foresman.

Scheman, N. (1996). Though this be method, yet there is madness in it: Paranoia and liberal epistemology. In E. F. Keller & H. Longino (Eds.), *Feminism and science* (pp. 203–219). New York: Oxford University Press.

Science and Innovation Advisory Council. (2001). *New Zealanders—innovators to the world: Turning great ideas into great ventures—a proposed innovation framework for New Zealand*. Report to the Prime Minister, August. (Available at http://www.siac.govt.nz/innovation/framework.pdf)

Scott, J. (2003). Deconstructing equality-versus-difference: Or, the uses of poststructuralist theory for feminism. In C. McCann & S. K. Kim (Eds.), *Feminist theory reader: Local and global perspectives* (pp. 378–391). New York: Routledge.

Seidman, S. (1983). *Liberalism and the origins of European social theory*. Berkeley, CA: University of California Press.

Seller, A. (1988). Realism versus relativism: Towards a politically adequate epistemology. In M. Griffiths & M. Whitford (Eds.), *Feminist perspectives in philosophy* (pp. 169–186). London: Macmillan.

Senge, P. (1990). *The fifth discipline: The art and practice of learning*. New York: Doubleday.

Senge, P., Cambron-McCabe, N., Lucas, T., Smith, B., Dutton, J., & Kleiner, A. (2000). *Schools that learn: A fifth discipline fieldbook for educators, parents, and everyone who cares about education*. New York: Currency/Doubleday.

Shapin, S. (1994). *A social history of truth: Civility and science in 17th century England*. Chicago, IL: Chicago University Press.

Shuker, R. (1987). *The one best system? A revisionist history of state schooling in New Zealand*. Palmerston North: Dunmore Press.

Siegel, H. (1980). Critical thinking as an educational ideal. *The Educational Forum*, *45*(1), 7–23.

Siegel, H. (1988). *Educating reason*. New York: Routledge.

Skilton-Silvester, P. (2003). Less like a robot: A comparison of change in an inner-city school and a Fortune 500 company. *American Educational Research Journal*, *40*(1), 3–41.

Slater, G. (1968). *The English peasantry and the enclosure of common fields*. New York: A. M. Kelley.

Slaughter, R. (1989). Cultural reconstruction in the post-modern world. *Journal of Curriculum Studies*, *21*(3), 255–270.

Slavin, R. (1996). Success for all: A summary of research. *Journal of Education for Students Placed at Risk*, *1*, 41–76.

Slavin, R., Madden, N., Dolan, L., Wasik, B., Ross, S., & Smith, L. (1994). "Whenever and wherever we choose..." The replication of success for all. *Phi Delta Kappan*, *75*, 639–647.

Smith, E. (2003). Failing boys and moral panics: Perspectives on the under-achievement debate. *British Journal of Educational Studies*, *51*(3), 282–295.

Solomon, J. (2002). Science stories and science texts: What can they do for our students? *Studies in Science Education*, *37*, 85–106.

Spivak, G. (1989). Feminism and deconstruction, again: Negotiating with unacknowledged masculinism. In T. Brennan (Ed.), *Between feminism and psychoanalysis* (pp. 206–223). NewYork: Routledge.

Stehr, N. (1994). *Knowledge societies*. London: Sage.

Sternberg, R. (1996). *Successful intelligence: How practical and creative intelligence determine life*. New York: Simon and Schuster.

Stewart, T. (1997). *Intellectual capital: The new wealth of nations*. New York: Doubleday.

Street, B. (1984). *Literacy in theory and practice*. Cambridge, UK: Cambridge University Press.

Street, B. (1995). *Social literacies: Critical approaches to literacy in development, ethnography and education*. London: Longman.

Sutch, W. B. (1961). *Education for New Zealand's future*. Wellington: Department of Industries and Commerce.

Tawney, R. (1912). *The agrarian problem in the 16th century*. London: Longmans Green.

Teese, R. (1989). Australian private schools, specialisation and curriculum conservation. *British Journal of Educational Studies, 37*(3), 235–252.

Thomson, P. (2002). *Schooling the rustbelt kids*. Sydney, NSW: Allen and Unwin.

Thrupp, M. (1999). *Schools making a difference—let's be realistic! School mix, school effectiveness, and the social line of reform*. Buckingham, UK: Open University Press.

Thrupp, M. (2000). Compensating for class: Are school improvement researchers being realistic? *Education and Social Justice*, 2(2), 2–11.

Thrupp, M., Mansell, H., Hawksworth, L., & Harold, B. (2003). "Schools can make a difference": But do teachers, heads and governors really agree? *Oxford Review of Education*, 29(4), 471–484.

Thurow, L. (1996). *The future of capitalism: How today's economic forces will shape tomorrow's world*. New York: William Morrow.

Toffler, A. (1970). *Future shock*. London: Bodley Head.

Toulmin, S. (1999). Knowledge as shared procedures. In Y. Engestrom, R. Miettinen, & R. Punamaki (Eds.), *Perspectives on activity theory* (pp. 53–65). Cambridge, UK: Cambridge University Press.

Touraine, A. (1971). *The post-industrial society: Tomorrow's social history—classes, conflicts and culture in the programmed society*. New York: Random House.

Traweek, S. (1988). *Beamtimes and lifetimes: The world of high-energy physics*. Cambridge, MA: Harvard University Press.

Traweek, S. (1989). *Particle physics culture*. Cambridge, MA: Harvard University Press.

Trinh Minh-ha, T. (1988). Not like you/like you: Colonial women and the interlocking questions of identity and difference. *Inscriptions, 3*(4), 71–79.

Tuana, N. (1989). *Feminism and science.* Bloomington, IN: Indiana University Press.

Turkle, S. (1997). *Life on the screen: Identity in the age of the Internet.* London: Phoenix.

Turnbull, D. (1984). Relativism, reflexivity and the sociology of scientific knowledge. *Metascience, 1*(2), 47–60.

Tyack, D. (1974). *The one best system? A history of American urban education.* Cambridge, MA: Harvard University Press.

Varela, F., Thompson, E., & Rosch, E. (1991). *The embodied mind: Cognitive science and human experience.* Cambridge, MA: MIT Press.

Vygotsky, L. (1986). *Thought and language.* Cambridge, MA: MIT Press.

Walkerdine, V. (1984). Developmental psychology and the child-centred pedagogy. In J. Henriques, W. Hollway, C. Urwin, C. Venn, & V. Walkerdine (Eds.), *Changing the subject: Psychology, social regulation and subjectivity* (pp. 153–202). London: Methuen.

Walkerdine, V. (1988). *The mastery of reason.* London: Routledge.

Walkerdine, V. (1989). *Counting girls out.* London: Virago.

Walkerdine, V. (1997). *Daddy's girl: Young girls and popular culture.* London: Macmillan.

Walkerdine, V., & Lucey, H. (1989). *Democracy in the kitchen: Regulating mothers and socialising daughters.* London: Virago.

Walkerdine, V., Lucey, H., & Melody, J. (2001). *Growing up girl: Psychosocial explorations of gender and class.* London: Palgrave.

Walzer, M. (1983). *Spheres of justice: A defense of pluralism and equality.* Oxford: Blackwell.

Ward, G., & Haigh, M. (2000, July). *Exploring the nature of science though historical case studies.* Paper presented at the twelfth biennial conference of the New Zealand Association of Science Educators, Massey University, Palmerston North.

Ward, S. (1996). *Reconfiguring truth: Post-modernism, science studies and the search for a new model of knowledge*. New York: Rowman and Littlefield.

Ward, S. (1997). Being objective about objectivity: The ironies of standpoint epistemological critiques of science. *Sociology, 31*, 773–791.

Weis, L. (1990). *Working class without work: High school students in a de-industrialising economy*. New York: Routledge.

Weis, L. (2003). Gender, masculinity and the new economy. *Australian Educational Researcher, 30*(3), 111–129.

Weis, L., & Fine, M. (2000). *Construction sites: Excavating race, class and gender among urban youth*. New York: Teachers College Press.

Weis, L., & Fine, M. (2004). *Working method: Social injustice and social research*. New York: Routledge.

Whitty, G. (1985). *Sociology and school knowledge: Curriculum theory, research and politics*. London: Methuen.

Whitty, G., & Young, M. (Eds.). (1976). *Explorations in the politics of school knowledge*. Driffield, UK: Studies in Education Ltd.

Willis, P. (1977). *Learning to labour: How working class boys get working class jobs*. Farnborough, UK: Saxon House.

Wilson. K. (2001). Exclusive rights, enclosure and the patenting of life. In B. Tokar (Ed.), *Redesigning life? The worldwide challenge to genetic engineering* (pp. 290–296). London: Zed Books.

Wittgenstein, L. (1969). *On certainty*. New York: Harper Torchbooks.

Wittgenstein, L. (1972). *Philosophical investigations*. Oxford: Blackwell.

Woolgar, S. (1981). Interests and explanation in the social study of science. *Social Studies of Science, 11*, 365–394.

Woolgar, S. (1988). *Science: The very idea*. London: Tavistock.

World Bank. (2003). *Lifelong learning in the global knowledge economy*. Washington DC: Author.

Yates, L. (1997). Gender equity and the boys debate: What sort of a challenge is it? *British Journal of Sociology of Education, 18*(3), 337–347.

Yeatman, A. (1993). Voice and representation in the politics of difference. In S. Gunew & A. Yeatman (Eds.), *Feminism and the politics of difference* (pp. 228–245). Sydney: Allen & Unwin.

Yeatman, A. (1994). *Postmodern revisionings of the political*. New York: Routledge.

Yeatman, A. (2000). *Mutual obligation and the ethics of individualised citizenship*. Online opinion retrieved 21 April 2001 from www.onlineopinion.com.au/2000/dec00/Yeatman.htm

Yeatman, A., & Wilson, M. (Eds.). (1995). *Justice and identity: Antipodean practices*. Sydney, NSW: Allen and Unwin.

Young, I. M. (1990a). *Justice and the politics of difference*. Princeton, NJ: Princeton University Press.

Young, I. M. (1990b). The ideal of community and the politics of difference. In L. Nicholson (Ed.), *Feminism/postmodernism* (pp. 300–323). New York: Routledge.

Young, I. M. (1992). Together in difference: Transforming the logic of group political conflict. *Political Theory Newsletter*, *4*, 11–27.

Young, M. (Ed.). (1971). *Knowledge and control: New directions in the sociology of education*. London: Collier Macmillan.

Ziman, J. (2000). *Real science*. Cambridge, UK: Cambridge University Press.

ALSO AVAILABLE FROM NZCER

Beyond the Age of Aquarius: Reframing alternative education

Karen Vaughan

Beyond the Age of Aquarius: Reframing alternative education examines the way in which alternative schools and initiatives from the 1960s, 1970s, and contemporary times share a progressive "frame" of ideas. The fascinating analysis shows how many of these initiatives have been reinvented into a schooling system where alternatives can exist within the mainstream – as individualised education "pathways" of potentially comparable status and boundless flexibility.

This book traces the shift from the radical alternative schooling movement of the 1960s and 1970s; and from the progressive ideas of democratic schools and child-centred teaching. While many schools of that era have disappeared, others have integrated into a new orthodoxy of diversity.

Alternatives still pose powerful challenges to schooling but these no longer involve claiming "alternative" status. Only "at-risk" youth programmes are now recognised as Alternative Education (AE) in New Zealand.

Beyond the Age of Aquarius is a consideration of the transformation of the practices, spaces, and regulation of schooling, and is designed to provoke discussion on the role and "fit" of alternatives in schooling in relation to the mainstream

NZCER 2004   ISBN 1-877293-41-5   RRP $27.00

ORDER FROM

NZCER Sales, PO Box 3237, Wellington
Phone: 04 802 1450   Fax: 04 384 7933
Email: sales@nzcer.org.nz

A full list of NZCER publications is available on the Internet. Check out our site at www.nzcer.org.nz